Roots in the Cotton Patch

Roots in the Cotton Patch

THE CLARENCE JORDAN SYMPOSIUM 2012

edited by
Kirk and Cori Lyman-Barner

VOLUME ONE

CASCADE *Books* • Eugene, Oregon

ROOTS IN THE COTTON PATCH
The Clarence Jordan Symposium 2012, Volume One

Copyright © 2014 Wipf and Stock Publishers. All rights reserved. Except for brief quotations in critical publications or reviews, no part of this book may be reproduced in any manner without prior written permission from the publisher. Write: Permissions, Wipf and Stock Publishers, 199 W. 8th Ave., Suite 3, Eugene, OR 97401.

Cascade Books
An Imprint of Wipf and Stock Publishers
199 W. 8th Ave., Suite 3
Eugene, OR 97401

www.wipfandstock.com

ISBN 13: 978-1-62032-985-6

Cataloguing-in-Publication data:

Roots in the cotton patch : the Clarence Jordan symposium 2012, volume one / edited by Kirk and Cori Lyman-Barner; with a foreword by Tony Campolo.

xvi + 174 pp. ; 23 cm. Includes bibliographical references.

ISBN 13: 978-1-62032-985-6

1. Jordan, Clarence. 2. Koinonia Farm—History. I. Title.

BV4407.67 R1 2014

Manufactured in the U.S.A.

Contents

Foreword—Tony Campolo   *vii*

Preface—Lenny Jordan   *ix*

Introduction—Kirk Lyman-Barner   *xi*

Opening Remarks for the Clarence Jordan Symposium
—President Jimmy Carter   *xiii*

Part One: *Arts and Storytelling*

1. Cotton Patch Gospel: The Local Theology and Folk Art of Clarence Jordan's Preaching—*Leonora Tubbs Tisdale*   3

2. The Cotton Patch Versions: Why Do We Love Them So Much?—*Ann Coble*   23

Part Two: *Grace and Healing*

3. Clarence Jordan as a (White) Interpreter of the Bible—*Greg Carey*   33

4. Strangers in a Strange Land: Alternative Christian Voices in the South—*Timothy Downs*   44

5. Clarence Jordan as Baptist: Celebrating the Radical Baptist Heritage—*G. W. Carlson*   50

6. At Work in the Fields of the Lord: Clarence Jordan as Prophet of Radical Ordinariness—*Charles Marsh*   83

7. "Loving Respect, Clear Disagreement"—*Vincent Harding with John Pierce*   99

8. Spittin' Image of the Almighty—*Joyce Hollyday*   105

Contents

Part Three: *Community*

9   Reflections on Florence Kroeger Jordan (1912–1987)
    —*Linda Fuller Degelmann*   121

10 Memories of My Mother, Florence—*Jim Jordan*   128

11 Koinonia Co-founder Martin England—Insurance Guy
    —*Dave Willis*   130

12 Reflections on the Americus Movement
    —*Sam Mahone*   134

13 Baptized in the Spit—*Greg Wittkamper*   140

14 In Scorn of the Consequences—*Dallas Lee*   144

Afterword—Bren Dubay   153

Celebrating the Life and Ministry of Clarence Jordan: A Working Bibliography—G. W. Carlson   157

Contributors   169

Foreword

Clarence Jordan was as conservative as the Word of God, and as liberal as the love of God. He was conservative because he took the Bible seriously and, like an old-time Baptist preacher, could quote chapter and verse to support his vision for Koinonia Farm. To most people in the racially segregated South, Clarence Jordan seemed to be the epitome of what defined liberalism as he called Christians to live and work together in intentional community, embracing each other across racial lines at a time when such behavior was counter-cultural. His model for Koinonia Farm was derived from the second chapter of Acts, which reads, "All who believed were together and had all things in common; they would sell their possessions and goods, and distribute the proceeds to all, as any had need" (Acts 2:44–45 NRSV).

Those who lived at Koinonia Farm were committed to abandoning America's affluent, consumeristic lifestyle, and believed that we all should live simply so that others might simply live.

In the midst of World War II, those who joined with Clarence Jordan embraced nonviolence as the way to resist evildoers, as taught in the Sermon on the Mount. This made them seem unpatriotic to many of their critics. And long before environmentalism was in vogue, they made living in harmony with nature part of what Clarence would call "The God Movement."

Jordan was irked by the ways in which mammon had sapped the church of its prophetic ministry. Fear as to how speaking out against racism and other social injustices would impact their financial security and popularity had led far too many preachers to give a watered down gospel from their pulpits. It is no wonder that so many compromised clergy deemed Jordan their enemy.

The good news is that more than seventy years later the message of Koinonia Farm and Clarence Jordan lives on and continues to grow. All across America, and even overseas, there are intentional communities

Foreword

springing up, drawing to them thousands of Christians, and especially young Christians, who want to live out the radical teachings of Jesus, and be the kind of church that was envisioned by those first century Christians, of whom it was said, "they turned the world upside down." In the essays that follow, you will meet some of them and read how their lives were impacted by Clarence Jordan and Koinonia Farm. These essays are printed versions of presentations made at the first Clarence Jordan Symposium in Americus, Georgia. I know many of the presenters and I know they are "for real." What follows is a presentation of authentic Christianity.

Tony Campolo
Eastern University

Preface

When I heard about Koinonia Farm's vision for the 2012 Celebration and the request that I serve as chair, I did not hesitate. After a twelve-year departure from the original vision, Koinonia Farm had, in 2005 under the leadership of Bren Dubay, returned to its roots as an intentional Christian community. I was inspired and loved what I was seeing.

It was clear to me why a Clarence Jordan Symposium would be one of the major events of the Celebration. Those at the farm knew the history and the legacy. They felt an obligation to share them and pass them on to future generations. Even with the overwhelming amount of day-in-and-day-out work they performed, they had taken the time to water their roots. It only made sense that a Symposium emerge as a new fruit of Koinonia Farm.

Once more, out of a small group of people comes something of tremendous worth. Following the violence and economic boycott of the 1950s and early 1960s, full membership in the community dwindled to just six adults in 1963, but the foundation on which my parents, Clarence and Florence Jordan, and Martin and Mabel England founded Koinonia (from the Greek meaning fellowship, communion, holding all things in common) was not one based on numbers. From the beginning, the size of the community was not the intention of their "intentional" community.

It may surprise some to know that there are only six full members today. They are rebuilding a way of life at Koinonia Farm started in 1942. Some folks believe that in the late 1960s my father turned away from the idea of intentional community. My mother addressed this on multiple occasions during her lifetime and I add my voice to hers: "Clarence Jordan never gave up on community." He explored other options during a particularly hard time, but he always came back to the idea that however small or whatever direction he felt led by God, it would involve living in the way the early church lived—in intentional community. He always returned to the notion of the koinonia and this place called Koinonia Farm. Giving up on community was something that was non-negotiable for him, even in the hardest, darkest days in Koinonia's history.

Preface

So from these efforts come the 2012 Clarence Jordan Symposium and these two books: *Roots in the Cotton Patch* and *Fruits of the Cotton Patch*. Koinonia Stewards Bren Dubay, Norris Harris, Kathleen Monts, Elizabeth Dede, Brendan and Sarah Prendergast, and I sincerely thank all the contributors to these books—the theologians, artists, academicians, peace makers, farmers, etc., who, touched by Clarence Jordan and Koinonia Farm, agreed to participate. Each one spoke eloquently and made the Symposium an event that will not be forgotten by those in attendance. Now you as reader can share in the experience or relive it if you were there.

We acknowledge with sincere gratitude the tremendous job Kirk Lyman-Barner did as chair of the 2012 Clarence Jordan Symposium. He expanded the vision and worked the details masterfully. He and his wife, Cori, served as editors of the two Symposium books. They have done magnificent work.

We thank, too, Kat Mournighan, a supporting member of Koinonia Farm, and Amanda Moore, a novice in the community, whose behind the scenes efforts along with all who helped them assured a joyous and thought-provoking occasion. For all who supported and attended the Symposium, thank you. A special thanks to The Fuller Center for Housing, Habitat for Humanity, and the Bruderhof Community for all they contributed to assure the success of this monumental endeavor.

All went so well that we are planning for the next Clarence Jordan Symposium to be held in March 2017, the year the community turns seventy-five. We are honored to have Jonathan Wilson-Hartgrove serve as chair of the event.

The Jordan family rejoices over the success of the Symposium, the publication of these books, and at what's happening at Koinonia Farm. Come and see.

Lenny Jordan
Franklin, North Carolina
April 2013

Introduction

In a conversation with Koinonia Farm Director Bren Dubay, I learned that the anniversary of Clarence and Florence Jordan's 100th birthdays was rolling around. It would also be the seventieth anniversary of the founding of Koinonia Farm. Intrigued, I suggested that we have a Symposium similar to the Christianity and Democracy conference President Carter spoke at in 1991 at Emory University. As a young student at Pittsburgh Theological Seminary I had the privilege of attending this event and I proposed to Bren that we owed the next generation a similar type of gathering.

Words cannot describe my excitement when Bren liked the idea, and within a few short weeks, our neighbors in Plains, President and Mrs. Carter, agreed to be honorary chairs. Together we envisioned a gathering of people who have been influenced by Clarence, including theologians, activists, farmers, entrepreneurs, and performing artists who would present papers connecting their work to Clarence's life and example. The final celebration would be the publication of those presentations in this book.

Clarence wrote a lot about partnerships. In his famous 1968 letter he wrote,

> It has also become clear to us that as man has lost his identity with God he has lost it with his fellow man. We fiercely compete with one another as if we were enemies, not brothers. We want only to kill human beings for whom Christ died. Our cities provide us anonymity, not community. Instead of partners, we are aliens and strangers. Greed consumes us, and self-interest separates us and confines us to ourselves or our own group.
>
> As a result, the poor are being driven from rural areas; hungry, frustrated, angry masses are huddled in the cities; suburbanites walk in fear; the chasm between blacks and whites grows wider and deeper; war hysteria invades every nook and cranny of the earth.
>
> We must have a new spirit—a spirit of partnership with one another.

Clarence's ideas of Partnership Housing and The Fund for Humanity caused a revolution. They intrigued Millard Fuller, who called Clarence his

Introduction

"Spiritual Father" and who revolutionized philanthropy with Habitat for Humanity. No longer would Christians simply write a check to missionaries doing the Lord's work in far off lands. Instead they would pick up hammers, trowels and caulk guns and do the kingdom work themselves. Indeed, every nail that is driven and every block that is laid in a wall became a testimony to the legacy of Clarence Jordan and the people he inspired.

And Koinonia Farm continues today to ask for help "shipping the nuts out of Georgia," Clarence's slogan for his pecan mail-order business that sustained the farm during the racial boycott. They also do so much more, from practicing and teaching permaculture farming and design, to living a new monastic life of community, and hosting a robust intern program.

Clarence would be the first to say that an endeavor the magnitude of the Symposium is not the work of any one person. Special thanks need first to go to Bren Dubay for not running the other direction when I proposed this undertaking, and for giving legs to the vision which became the Symposium. Sincere gratitude goes to David Snell, President of the Fuller Center for Housing, who gave his blessing to my time and focus on this celebration. The collaborative efforts of the Koinonia Farm community members, Lenny Jordan, and the dedicated staff at Habitat for Humanity International made the experience both professional and profound. My beautiful partner and bride Cori gave amazing suggestions and edits throughout this entire project. Ted Lewis of Wipf and Stock has been a magnanimous coach over the many months of compiling the presentations and I can't thank his team enough for publishing this important body of work.

I love Clarence's translation of Peter organizing the first Christian community partnerships after Jesus was resurrected: "Rock said to them, 'Reshape your lives, and let each of you be initiated into the family of Jesus Christ so your sins can be dealt with; and you will receive the free gift of the Holy Spirit. For the guarantee is to you and your relatives, as well as to all the outsiders whom the Lord our God shall invite.' Rock was going down on other matters, too, and kept urging them on. 'Save yourselves,' he was telling them, 'from this goofed-up society.'"

Our society is still goofed-up. But I have hope because of the story of the life of Clarence Jordan and the Koinonia Farm experiment. The answer is found in the teachings of Jesus and life lived in partnership with God and community. Millard Fuller once told me that Clarence often prayed for the interpreters of Scripture. It is your turn to interpret this grand story.

Kirk Lyman-Barner, Chair
2012 Clarence Jordan Symposium

Opening Remarks for the Clarence Jordan Symposium

President Jimmy Carter

I know there are dozens of people here who can make a better presentation than I can about Clarence Jordan. I know his children are here, his grandchildren are here, his brothers and sisters and in-laws are here. But I've been asked tonight just to give a few remarks about what Clarence Jordan meant to me personally and to this region of the state of Georgia, to the United States of America and to the world.

I was thinking, as I prepared my remarks, that in a lifetime of existence, there are very few great people that we ever meet. And of course as some of you may remember, I've been President of the United States. I've known some great men: Anwar Sadat, who helped bring peace to Israel and Egypt; Nelson Mandela, who still works with me in a group called The Elders. We visit him when we go to South Africa. But I also remember on an equal basis, Millard Fuller and Clarence Jordan.

I was coming into the theater a few minutes ago and I found a Walk of Fame inscription there with Clarence Jordan's name on it. I looked at some of the other names, and it was kind of ironic because I remember some of the other names who are inscribed in the front were partially responsible at least, or condoned, the bombs, the bullets, and the fires that tried to destroy what Clarence Jordan created at Koinonia. And finally, as you know, during the 1950s, he was forced to begin selling pecans by the mail since his store on U.S. Highway 19 was burned down, bombed. And he developed the phrase, "Help us ship the nuts out of Georgia."

I think in many ways that prediction has come true, because a lot of the nuts that were in Georgia then and tried to burn down Koinonia have been converted by Clarence Jordan into supporters of what he stood for. And I'm very grateful for that.

The first time we ever saw Clarence Jordan personally was the night that my wife, who was a Methodist, joined the Baptist church. We were having a revival at the Plains Baptist Church and just before the sermon began, Clarence Jordan came in because he was a friend of our revival speaker. I would guess that about a third of the people there got up and walked out, because those were times when it was not a common or acceptable thing for anyone to maintain that African American citizens were equal to white citizens in the eyes of our government or in the eyes of God. This was a difficult time for Koinonia.

I later knew Clarence as an uncle of Hamilton Jordan. Hamilton Jordan helped to shape my life. When I ran for governor the first time in 1966, Hamilton volunteered to help me—both he and his future wife, Nancy. He ran my campaign for governor in 1970 and he ran my campaign for President in 1976. I would never have been governor or President without him. I remember Clarence's brother, Robert Jordan, who was Chief Justice of the Georgia Supreme Court. And so I think that the fine heritage of the Jordan family is still present and active in this country and around the world.

Clarence Jordan showed an early courage. As you all know, in 1942 he and two Baptist missionaries started Koinonia. It's good for us to remember that this was six years before President Harry Truman ordained, as Commander in Chief, that all the military men and women would no longer be bound by racial discrimination. I was an officer on a submarine, and in 1948, that had a major impact on my life. I saw the benefits of what Harry Truman did, and it was condemned, not only in the South, but by the Congress and by many others. And what Clarence Jordan did was not only six years before Truman, it was thirteen years before Rosa Parks sat in the front of a bus in Montgomery, Alabama, and before Martin Luther King, Jr., became famous.

It was not an accident that Clarence got a degree in agriculture from the University of Georgia in 1933 and a few years later got a degree in Greek New Testament, a PhD, as a matter of fact. He started, as has already been mentioned, a "demonstration plot" for God's kingdom.

He founded Koinonia on four basic principles: nonviolence; equality of all people; protecting the ecology of the world; and common ownership. I really didn't have much to do with Clarence until I became a member of the Sumter County School Board. But I had been listening to what he said. When I got on the school board, I suggested that all the school board

Opening Remarks for the Clarence Jordan Symposium

members—there were only five of us then, appointed by the grand jury—would go around and visit all the schools in Sumter County. All five of us, of course, were white. And the others decided reluctantly to go and visit all the schools. We found twenty-three schools for black children. And they were in the basements of churches or in the front rooms of houses. The school books were all handed down after they were worn out by the white students. I remember going to one place out in Archery, where I lived, and teenage boys were sitting on little, tiny chairs about eight inches wide, that were made for little children.

Finally, though, we had to acknowledge that the black children had so many schools because they didn't have any school buses. So we began to consolidate the schools. And we had to provide school buses. But the state legislature passed a law that any school bus hauling African American children had to have the front fenders painted black so everybody would know who was in the buses.

I say these things not to condemn the society in which I grew up as a boy, but just to point out how far things have come. Later, since I had known Clarence and he had helped me with my school board business, I tried to go down and sell him some fertilizer and seed. He said, "Jimmy, I can buy it cheaper than you can." So I couldn't sell him fertilizer, I couldn't sell him feed, I couldn't sell him seed, but they had peanuts to be shelled and I had a peanut shelling plant, so I was very proud to shell Koinonia's peanuts.

Clarence had kind of a quiet resolve. He understood the problems of the school board, trying to deal with the children in a mixed community at Koinonia, both his children and others and African American children. He maintained his equanimity; he didn't join the civil rights movement and its public demonstrations. But he lived the essence of civil rights.

And then he wrote *The Cotton Patch Gospel*, as all of you know. I have a copy on my desk at the Carter Center always. And it was a shock to me, a revelation to me, but now I began to equate the crucifixion with lynching. And I began to bring the Holy Land into Georgia. Those kinds of things were heartwarming, but also stretched our hearts and minds to look on the resurrection and incarnation of Christ not just as an invitation someday to go to heaven, but, as Clarence would say, it was to indicate God's presence permanently with us.

At The Carter Center now, where Rosalyn and I work, we try to emulate the teachings of Clarence Jordan. In 2008 I helped organize what's called a New Baptist Covenant. It's a remnant of the earliest Baptist organization

Opening Remarks for the Clarence Jordan Symposium

in America. It was called a Tri-annual Convention, where all the Baptists came together, both black and white and others, every three years in Philadelphia. But in 1845 that Tri-annual Convention was destroyed because the Southern Baptists decided they did not want to participate and worship God anymore with African Americans. So we resurrected that concept. And in 2008 we began having the New Baptist Covenant meet every three years. And we had 15,000 people the first night in Atlanta. A little over half of them were African American and the others were white. There was never a sense of disharmony or inequality and all during that night, I thought about Clarence Jordan. In 2011 we had another one. We were thinking about the tremendous changes that are taking place, not only among Baptists, but among all Christians. No longer are the churches the last holdouts in bringing about the integration and equality of the races.

I think the permanent, historic significance of Koinonia has been demonstrated vividly by the founding of Habitat for Humanity there, and then later, the Fuller Center for Housing, and earlier, Jubilee Partners were there. The Fullers and Don Mosley, who heads up Jubilee Partners, are here tonight.

In a few weeks, my wife and I will be going to Haiti. This will be our twenty-ninth year working for Habitat for Humanity. We'll be building 100 homes in Haiti to fill out a 500-home village in the epicenter of the earthquake. So I've learned to remember, in somewhat brutal terms, what life was like for me and other Georgians and other Americans, before Clarence Jordan came along—how much life has been transformed, secular life and religious life, because he lived. I'm very proud tonight to help honor this great man.

PART ONE

Arts and Storytelling

1

Cotton Patch Gospel

The Local Theology and Folk Art of Clarence Jordan's Preaching

Leonora Tubbs Tisdale

In my own research and writing as a teacher and scholar of preaching, I have primarily focused on two areas of interest: *contextual preaching*—that is, preaching that stays close to the ground of its hearers in both its theology (the themes, issues, and concerns it addresses) and its art (the language, forms, examples and illustrations that it employs), and *prophetic preaching*—proclamation that challenges the status quo in light of the counter-cultural witness of the scriptures.

Frankly, I can think of no one who embodies *both* of those aspects of preaching better than Clarence Jordan. Jordan's preaching is highly contextual, exemplifying what I mean when I use the phrase "preaching as local theology and folk art" (the title of my first book). His Cotton Patch gospel addresses topics such as racism, consumerism, militarism, and the tendency of the church to overly spiritualize Jesus, all the while doing so in the folk idiom of southwest Georgia farmers. John the Baptizer is depicted as being dressed in blue jeans and a leather jacket, living on corn bread and collard greens, and "dipping" people in the Chattahoochee River. The "God Movement" is compared to a "jeweler looking for special pearls" who, "when he finds a super-duper one... goes and unloads his whole stock and buys that pearl." And Judas, after "squealing" on Jesus, tells the archbishops and elders that he had "ratted on an innocent man."[1]

But Jordan's proclamation is also highly prophetic, bringing the scriptures to bear upon current issues in church and society in ways that challenge and upend and often offend his hearers. He believes in a radical Jesus, and he believes Jesus is serious when he calls his followers to live just as radically themselves. For Jordan there is no explaining away the Sermon on the Mount. Christians are called to embrace its teachings and to model their lives after Jesus' own, even if it costs them dearly.

In this presentation I will delve more deeply into the genius of both the prophetic local theology and the folk art of Jordan's preaching and teaching. My focus will be on the entire corpus of Jordan's published works, since I firmly believe that he "preached" as much in his Cotton Patch versions of the Bible and his Sermon on the Mount Bible study as he did in his sermons. There is also a symbiotic relationship between Jordan's sermons and his Cotton Patch translations since the whole Cotton Patch endeavor began with Jordan translating scripture passages on which he planned to preach.[2]

I will be guided by several questions as I undertake this task. First, in terms of prophetic local theology, what are the key theological themes and social justice issues that Jordan addresses in his preaching and teaching, and what does he say about them? Second, in terms of folk art, what are the particular strategies Jordan employs to make his Cotton Patch gospel come to life in down-to-the ground and highly contextual ways?

My hope is that this study will contribute not only to a deeper understanding of the skill, insight and courage of this remarkable preacher of the gospel, but will also assist other preachers and teachers and writers in

---

1. Jordan, *The Cotton Patch Version of Matthew and John* (New York: Association Press), 1970.

2. Edward McDowell, who had been an instructor in Greek at Southern Seminary in Louisville when Clarence Jordan enrolled as a student, discusses the relation between the Cotton Patch translations and Jordan's preaching in his "Introduction" to Clarence Jordan, *The Cotton Patch Version of Hebrews and the General Epistles* (New York: Association Press, 1973), 11. He also says that many of the individual works of the New Testament that Jordan translated were widely circulated in pamphlet form before his first volume, *The Cotton Patch Version of Paul's Epistles*, was published.

discerning how they might become more effective contextual proclaimers of God's prophetic Word as well.

Central Themes in Jordan's Local Prophetic Theology

Race and Racism

One of the most striking things about Jordan's preaching is how central and predominant the themes of race and racism are to it. For Jordan, the church is called to be a community of racial equality and justice on this earth, and when it fails to do so, it radically fails its mission and purpose under God. Throughout the Pauline letters (Jordan's first published Cotton Patch volume), Jordan translates "Jew and Gentile" as "white man [sic] and Negro."[3] In the "Letter to the Christians in Birmingham (Ephesians)" he writes, "The Secret is that the Negroes are fellow partners and equal members, co-sharers in the privileges of the gospel of Jesus Christ."[4] In "The Letter to Christians in Washington (Romans)" he writes, "For not all Protestants are Protestants, and not all "good white folks" are *good* white folks . . . God's people are not the ones who give the appearance but whose lives are rooted in God's promises."[5] Significant, also, is the fact that Jordan addresses Philippians, the letter in which Paul expressed the most outward affection and love for a congregation, to the Alabaster African Church in Smithville, Alabama.

In the Cotton Patch version of Acts ("The Happenings"), after Cornwall (Cornelius), who is Black, greets the white Rock (Peter) as "mister," Rock replies, "Don't 'mister' me, for I am a human being the same as you." "I am convinced beyond any doubt . . . that God pays no attention to a man's skin. Regardless of his race, the man who respects God and practices justice is welcomed by him."[6] Timothy, Paul's co-worker, is depicted as being the son of "a very devout white woman" with a father who is a Negro.[7] And after

---

3. As Joyce Hollyday comments in her "Preface" to *Clarence Jordan: Essential Writings* (Maryknoll, NY: Orbis, 2003), "As to Clarence's use of 'Negro' and "Negroes': Although other terms are preferred today, these were considered appropriate and respectful in his time," 12.

4. Ibid., 108.

5. Ibid., 30–31.

6. Jordan, *The Cotton Patch Version of Luke and Acts: Jesus' Doings and the Happenings* (New York: Association Press, 1969), 115.

7. Ibid., 128–29.

Paul preaches a revival in Atlanta, the WAPs (White Anglo-Saxon Protestants) from Alabama "whipped up the people against him," saying, "Fellow southerners help us. This is the man who turns people everywhere against good white folks and the Bible and the church. And worse, he has even brought a nigger into the church and broke up our fine spirit of Christian unity and fellowship."[8]

Jesus, of course, is the key figure for Jordan in his theology of race. In Matthew, he retranslates the Isaiah suffering servant song that is quoted in this manner:

> See, my man whom I selected
> My loved one of whom I'm so proud.
> I will put my breath in him,
> And he will shout for justice for the black people.
> He won't wrangle and hassle,
> Nor make soapbox speeches.
> He won't even wring a chicken's neck,
> Or cut off a puppy's tail,
> Until he has won out in the fight for justice.
> His name will inspire hope in the black people.[9]

Jesus, in his teaching, holds up blacks as positive examples of the God Movement (such as when Jordan posits the Good Samaritan as a black man), and also welcomes and interacts freely with blacks as well as whites in his ministry (both the Syrophonecian and the Samaritan woman are black).

Closely aligned with Jordan's view of race and racism is his positing of the crucifixion of Christ as a lynching. He writes,

> . . . there just isn't any word in our vocabulary which adequately translates the Greek word for "crucifixion." Our crosses are so shined, so polished, so respectable that to be impaled on one of them would seem to be a blessed experience. We have thus emptied the term "crucifixion" of its original content of terrific emotion, of violence, of indignity and stigma, of defeat. I have translated it as "lynching," well aware that this is not technically correct. Jesus was officially tried and legally condemned, elements generally lacking in a lynching. But having observed the operation of Southern "justice," and at times having been its victim, I can testify that more people have been lynched "by judicial action" than by unofficial ropes.[10]

---

8. Ibid., 143.
9. Jordan, *Matthew and John*, 45.
10. Jordan, *The Cotton Patch Version of Paul's Epistles*, 8–9.

For Jordan the crucifixion was not something God pressed upon Jesus. It was something we humans did to Jesus because we could not abide his preaching and teaching. In his sermon "The Death of Jesus," Jordan proclaims, "I don't believe the crucifixion was the will of God . . . I think the kind of life [Jesus] lived was inevitably a life in the shadow of crucifixion. It was a life in such tension with the world . . . that either the world had to die or Jesus had to die."[11] "Jesus did die for our sins, and as a result of our sins. God made him available, but God didn't kill him. We did."[12]

The theme of race and racism is so prevalent in Jordan's writings that it often seems to function as the "key theme" around which all others gravitate. His own passion for the issue as well as his deep distress over the church's recalcitrance in following Jesus' model of radical inclusivity is nowhere more evident than in his sermon "The Mind of Christ in the Racial Conflict."

> The thing that just burns my heart out and that I can hardly bear is that the Supreme Court is making more pagans be Christian than the Bible is making Christians be Christians. I can hardly take it at times when the whole integration struggle is being fought, not in the household of God, but in the bus depots, sitting around Woolworth's counter, arguing over whether you can eat hamburger and drink Cokes together, when we ought to be sitting around Jesus' table drinking wine and eating bread together . . . If anybody has to bear the blame and guilt for all the sit-ins and all the demonstrations and all the disorder in the South, it is the whitewashed Christians who have had the word of God and have locked it up in their hearts and refused to do battle with it.[13]

Certainly at the heart of the radical witness of Koinonia Farm was its insistence from its founding in 1942 that blacks and whites should work together, eat together, worship together, and be paid equally. This insistence on racial equality and justice was not only preached by Jordan, but was lived out in the witness of the Koinonia community and was the stance that most offended many of the farm's white neighbors in rural southwest Georgia.

---

11. Jordan, "The Death of Jesus," in *The Substance of Faith and Other Cotton Patch Sermons* (Eugene, OR: Cascade, 2005), 170.

12. Ibid., 172.

13. Jordan, *The Substance of Faith and Other Cotton Patch Sermons*, 119.

Wealth and Poverty

Another founding principle of Koinonia was that Christians should not be held captive by wealth, but should give away all their material possessions and hold "all things in common" like the early church did (cf. Acts 2:44). Jordan explains and defends this vision in his discussion of "Blessed are the merciful" in the Sermon on the Mount. "By "the merciful" [Jesus] means *those who have an attitude of such compassion toward all people that they want to share gladly all they have with one another and with the world. If they have any money, they don't give till it hurts—they give till it's gone. To them, people are no longer beggars to whom one gives a part, but brothers and sisters with whom one shares all."*[14]

G. McLeod (Mac) Bryan gives eyewitness testimony to the very simple lifestyle which resulted from such intentional Christian living at Koinonia:

> Koinonia Farm would be no Golden Pond where affluent senior citizens could retire to be pampered . . . This was bare-bones living, based upon subsistence farming. The whole group possessed only one car, a broken-down vehicle used mostly for grocery shopping or hauling fertilizer. Nobody paid income taxes because there were no wages; besides, if the entirely yearly income of the farm were divided among the respective members, it would have been below the poverty level . . . Nobody had insurance policies, either for health or life, since they trusted altogether on the support of the community of faithful.[15]

Jordan's Cotton Patch translations consistently reflect a dismay with the materialism of his day, and especially with the way in which the Christian church had bought into it. As Dallas Lee puts it, "To Clarence, materialism was the devil on the loose in the church house—literally or figuratively, take your pick. He believed the 'grievous sin of wealth' had stunted the church's influence and blinded Christians to the immediacy of the gospel story; that is, God becoming [human] and living among us."[16]

Consequently Jordan's writings consistently call the church to task for its materialistic ways:
From the Epistle of James:

---

14. Jordan, *Sermon on the Mount* (Valley Forge, PA: Judson, 1970), 17–18.

15. G. McLeod Bryan, *Voices in the Wilderness: Twentieth-Century Prophets Speak to the New Millennium* (Macon, Ga: Mercer University Press, 1999), 58–59.

16. Dallas Lee, "Introduction" to Jordan, *The Substance of Faith and Other Cotton Patch Sermons*, 3.

And you rich guys, hold on a minute. Get ready to moan and groan because of the hardships coming on you. Your gadgets are all broken down and your pretty clothes are full of holes. Your stocks and bonds are worthless, and their certificates shall be evidence against you and will gnaw at your hearts like a flame. You piled them up for the Judgment Day.[17]

My brothers, never let any prejudice creep into the faith of our glorious Lord, Jesus Christ. For if a well-dressed person in expensive jewelry comes to your church, and then a poor fellow in rags comes, and you go out of your way to be nice to the well-dressed person and say to him, "Come over here and sit by me," and then you say to the poor man, "Stand over there, or go up to the balcony," don't you make distinctions in the fellowship and become parties to vicious prejudices? Listen here, my dear brothers, hasn't God chosen the poor in this world's goods to be rich in faith and to be full citizens in the spiritual order which he established for those who love him?[18]

From Matthew 21:12f.:

Then Jesus went into First Church, pitched out the whole finance committee, tore up the investment and endowment records, and scrapped the long-range expansion plans. "My house shall be known for its commitment to God," he shouted, "but you have turned it into a religious racket!"[19]

From Acts 17:16f:

Since *we* are *God's* stock, we ought never to think of the Deity in terms of budgets or statistics or buildings—the product of man's craft and cunning. God used to excuse people when they didn't know better, but now he's making it clear to all people everywhere that they've got to change their ways.[20]

Jordan makes it clear that people who are living in a way that is antithetical to the gospel are called to repent, which in Greek means "to change one's mind for the better, heartily to amend with abhorrence of one's past sins."[21]

17. Jordan, *The Cotton Patch Version of Hebrews and the General Epistles* (New York: Association Press, 1973), 146.

18. Jordan, "Letter of James" in *The Cotton Patch Version of Hebrews and the General Epistles*, 48–49.

19. Jordan, *Matthew and John*, 70–71.

20. Ibid., 133.

21. Jordan, *Sermon on the Mount*, 4.

He also emphasizes that Jesus calls us to a simpler, less materialistic lifestyle because he loves us and wants better for us. In a sermon entitled "Was Jesus Really Poor?" Jordan proclaims: "Jesus said, 'I don't want you to be money addicts. I want you to be healthy people.'"[22] "This is a liberating kind of thing. Jesus didn't want us shackled by the desire for things."[23] He goes on to affirm that if we trust God with our material lives, God will surely provide for us, just as he does "for the birds . . . the flowers . . . for everything that will let him."[24]

Jordan also makes clear the great reversal that will occur in the God Movement when the rich and powerful are brought down and the poor are lifted up. Mary, in the Magnificat, proclaims:

> From generation to generation
> His mercy showers those who fear him.
> With his strong arm
> He scatters the big boys
> Who think they're somebody.
> He pulls thrones from under the royalty
> And gives dignity to the lowly.
> He loads the hungry with good things
> But the rich he lets go with nothing at all.[25]

War and Peace

Clarence Jordan was a pacifist, and one of the themes that comes through in his preaching is his abhorrence of war and militarism. In Luke's Gospel, for example, John baptizes service men and tells them, "Don't ever use violence on anyone, and don't take advantage of native people—be satisfied with only your government check."[26] In the Sermon on the Mount, Jordan posits the Zealots as the group within the church who say, "Don't mope about the inner life. We must win our national freedom. Our hope is a mighty army."[27] In a sermon preached on the "three students" in the fiery furnace, he envisions all the people but the students falling "down on their

---

22. Jordan, "Was Jesus Really Poor?" in *The Substance of Faith and other Cotton Patch Sermons*, 86.
23. Ibid., 89.
24. Ibid., 90.
25. Jordan, *Luke and Acts*, 16, translation of Luke 2:50–53.
26. Jordan, *Luke and Acts*, 22, translation of Acts 3:14.
27. Jordan, *Sermon on the Mount*, 2.

faces when they heard the first strains of "The Stars and Stripes Forever," and comments, "In those days, you didn't burn your draft card; you got burnt."[28] And in a sermon preached on Jesus' call to us to love our enemies, Jordan proclaims:

> This seems to be the place that most of us really are at today. We love America, and limit our love to the shores and the boundaries of the United States. I think most of us reflect the idea that's inscribed on an old tombstone down in Mississippi. It says, "Here Lies J.H.S. In his lifetime he killed 99 Indians and lived in the blessed hope of making it 100, until he fell asleep in the arms of Jesus." Now Indians don't count. Ninety-nine of them, and you can live "in the blessed hope" of getting just one more to round it out as an even hundred and still fall asleep in the arms of Jesus. But if you had killed just one white man, you'd fall asleep in a noose. You see it's all right to kill Indians because we don't care about Indians, but you better not kill a white man. So a nation can drop an atom bomb on brown people, yellow people, and annihilate two whole cities of people and we give him the congressional medal. If he kills one man in the United States we give him the electric chair.[29]

Jordan also speaks out boldly against the underhanded tactics the US government used during his day on people who opposed its militaristic policies. For example, when "the seminary professors and denominational executives" plot to kill Jesus in Luke's Gospel, they hire detectives to pose as Christians and collect evidence from Jesus' preaching "so he could be arrested and turned over to the House Subversive Activities Committee."[30] And when the crowd takes Jesus to Pilate, they level these charges against him:

1. We have caught this fellow agitating our people.
2. He advocates the refusal to pay Federal taxes.
3. He claims to be the leader of a Movement.[31]

---

28. Jordan, "The Adventures of Three Students in a Fiery Furnace," in *The Substance of Faith*, 50.
29. Jordan, "The Lesson on the Mount—II," in *The Substance of Faith*, 75–76.
30. Jordan, *Luke and Acts*, 74.
31. Ibid., p. 82.

The Humanity of Jesus

From beginning to end, Jordan's gospel is intentionally grounded in a strong belief in the incarnation of Jesus Christ. For Jordan, Jesus was born in a real historical setting (when Augustus was President of the US and Herod was governor of Georgia), in a particular place (Gainesville), where he was placed in an apple crate, and where chicken farmers from the surrounding area came to pay him homage.[32] Jordan interprets the virgin birth as meaning "that God has decided to become a member of the human race, that he's joined with us, that he's blended his genes with our genes to produce a new kind of creature on this earth—a divine-human creature . . ."[33] And he interprets the resurrection "not as an invitation to us to come to heaven when we die, but as a declaration that [God] Himself has now established permanent, eternal residence on earth."[34]

While acknowledging that some people have taken offense at his theological approach because it makes Jesus "too contemporary and therefore too human, thus laying oneself open to charges of sacrilege and irreverence,"[35] Jordan defends it. "Jesus has been so zealously worshipped, his deity so vehemently affirmed, his halo so brightly illumined, and his cross so beautifully polished that in the minds of many he no longer exists as a man . . . Obviously this is not the thrust of the bible. Its emphasis all the way through is on the humanity of God—Immanuel, God with us; upon incarnation—the word become flesh, here and now, in our own experiences. Its movement is from heaven earthward, not vice versa.[36]

Jordan contends that the most dangerous heresy in which the church can engage is the gnostic heresy, in which we spiritualize Jesus, and do not acknowledge his true humanity.[37]

---

32. See Jordan, *Cotton Patch Version of Matthew and John*, 18–19.

33. Jordan, "The Humanity of God," in *The Substance of Faith and Other Cotton Patch Sermons*, 21–22.

34. Jordan, Ibid., 26.

35. Jordan, "Introduction" to *Cotton Patch Version of Luke and Acts*, 7.

36. Ibid., 7–8.

37. See Jordan's sermon "An Ancient Heresy Incarnate" in *The Substance of Faith*, 133–37.

Right Living, not Just Right Believing

According to Jordan, we humans are called to incarnate the gospel in our own lives by devoting ourselves to "The God Movement" (Jordan's phrase for the kingdom of God) here on earth. We learn how to do so through Jesus' teachings in the Sermon on the Mount, his "platform" for the movement. According to Jordan one of the biggest challenges facing Christians is to live into their commitment to follow Jesus as Lord—choosing to obey Jesus over all competing lords such as money, custom, or law. He contends that about 98 percent of believers profess faith in Jesus as Lord, but are lying since they do not acknowledge Jesus as such in their everyday lives.[38] Instead, Jordan calls us to embrace Jesus' "program" set forth for us in the Sermon on the Mount, and to enter fully into incarnating his life in our own lives. Like Nicodemus, we need to be "sired" from above, so that the Spirit dwells in us and we fully live into The God Movement in our everyday lives.[39]

Jordan is suspicious of all silver-tongued and well-educated orators who talk about an issue or study an issue, but do not follow Jesus' teachings in their daily lives. Frequently in his writings it is the theological students or seminary professors who misunderstand Jesus and want to domesticate him. Those who "get" Jesus and his message are those who live out his radical call to discipleship in their own living.

It is no accident then that Jordan felt the primary witness he was making in the world was the very manner in which he and the other Koinonia farm folk lived their lives in southwest Georgia. Their embrace of intentional Christian community marked by deep commitments to racial equality, a non-materialistic lifestyle, and a nonviolent response to the threats of their neighbors was, for Jordan, the very essence of what Jesus has called us to be and to do.

The Folk Artistry of Jordan's Preaching

In my book *Preaching as Local Theology and Folk Art*, I wrote: "Preaching as folk art encourages pastors to employ more 'folk speech'—the ordinary, everyday, language of local congregations—in their proclamation. The more the preacher can interpret Scripture and its symbols within the particular

---

38. Ibid., 99.
39. Jordan, "Metamorphosis," in *The Substance of Faith*, 105.

language of the congregational subculture—employing its peculiar idioms, turns of phrase, colloquialisms, and proverbial sayings—the more 'down to earth' the sermon will seem to a local community."[40]

Theologically a great deal is at stake here. As long as preachers employ a relatively inaccessible language and style of speech in the pulpit and do not accommodate to the speech of their hearers, they can give the impression: (a) that the only true teachers in faith are preachers, or other "learned ones," who have secret knowledge of and access to this holy jargon (thus perpetuating the gnostic heresy); (b) that the realm of the sacred is separate and distinct from the realm of the secular, and that it is impossible to speak of the holy in ordinary terms (thus denying the incarnation); or (c) that the preacher considers himself or herself to be culturally superior to the hearers, and is only willing to have genuine conversations in faith with those who can speak his or her language (thus denying the call to be servants of a servant Lord).[41]

Clarence Jordan, in my estimation, is the master of preaching as folk art. In the "Introduction" to *The Cotton Patch Version of Luke and Acts*, Jordan says that the whole purpose of the Cotton Patch approach to the scriptures "is to help the modern reader have the same sense of participation in them which the early Christians must have had."[42] In order to facilitate that participation, Jordan uses a number of effective strategies. Here I identify four of those strategies, giving examples of how Jordan utilizes them in his own preaching and writing.

1) Changing Biblical Names to Contemporary Names

In order both to contemporize and contextualize the scriptures for his southwest Georgia constituency, Jordan frequently changes the names of biblical places, characters, groups, and events in his Cotton Patch writings.

For example, throughout Jordan's writings certain cities and places in Georgia are equated with certain biblical cities and places: Nazareth becomes Valdosta, Bethlehem is Gainesville, Jerusalem is Atlanta, the Sea of Galilee is Lake Lanier, and the Mount of Olives is called The Peach Orchard.

---

40. Tisdale, *Preaching as Local Theology and Folk Art* (Minneapolis: Augsburg Fortress, 1997), 127.
41. Ibid., 128.
42. Jordan, *Luke and Acts*, 7.

Instead of saying "A certain man went down from Jerusalem to Jericho," (the beginning of the Good Samaritan story in Luke 25) Jordan writes: "a man was going up from Atlanta to Albany and some gangsters held him up . . ."[43] When telling the story of Jesus healing of the ten lepers, he says, "When [Jesus] was on his way to Atlanta, he went through the ghetto of Griffin, where he was met by ten winos who stood at a distance and yelled, 'Mister Jesus, have mercy on us!'"[44] When Paul hears the call to come over to Macedonia and help its people, the call comes from "the North." And when in recounting his own pedigree the apostle Paul says: "I am a Southerner, born in Tallahassee, Fla, but reared in this city. I was graduated from Georgia Tech and was about as straightlaced, dyed in the wool WAP as any of you here today. In fact, I was one of the ring leaders of those trying to stamp out the Way, trumping up charges against both men and women, as the White Citizens council will affirm."[45]

Sometimes Jordan's use of name changes can make his message quite pointed, as in his version of Jesus' "woe" sayings in Luke 10:13–15: "It will be hell for you, Columbus. It will be hell for you, Albany. If Berlin and London had seen so many evidences of God's activity as you have, they would have humbly changed their ways a long time ago. But Berlin and London will have it easier in the Judgment than you. And you, Savannah, do you think you'll be praised to the skies? You'll be sent to hell!"[46]

Jordan also doesn't hesitate to intertwine biblical places with contemporary places, moving back and forth across time and space. For example, at the end of Acts, Paul finally makes it to Rome. Then Jordan adds this note: "The scene changes, and Paul is once again our contemporary. He is in Washington to present his 'case' to the Supreme Court."[47]

Jordan also changes the names of people and groups. When Jesus appoints the twelve disciples ("twelve agents") in Matthew 10, their names are listed as follows: "first is Simon, who is called Rock, and Andy, his brother; Jim, Mr. Zebedee's boy, and his brother Jack; then Phil and Bart; Tom and Matt the revenuer; Jim Alphaeus and Tad; Simon the Rebel and Judas Iscariot, who turned him in."[48] The fishermen who are his disciples call Jesus

43. Ibid., 46.
44. Ibid., 66.
45. Jordan, *Luke and Acts*, 144 (comment on 22:1f.).
46. Ibid., 45.
47. Ibid., 158.
48. Jordan, *Matthew and John*, 38.

"Skipper!"[49] Zacchaeus is Zeke Geers. Zechariah is Zack Harris. Yet while many names are changed, some—like Mary, Elizabeth, Judas and Herod—remain the same. Jordan's criteria for doing so is not altogether clear.

In terms of the names given to groups, the Pharisees are church people; the scribes are theological professors; the Sadduccees are members of the Conservative Party. Sinners and tax collectors are Yankees (playing into Southern biases at the time). And the Chaldeans—who brought accusation against the Jews in the book of Daniel—are the John Besmirch Society!

In the Book of Acts, events are also renamed. Pentecost (the harvest festival) is referred to as "Thanksgiving Day." The Passover gathering of chief priests and scribes in Luke 22 is "the annual meeting, which is called the Convention."[50] And the Passover meal itself is referred to as "Alumni Banquets and Communion."

Even modes of travel are sometimes updated in Jordan's translations. For example, instead of traveling throughout the world by boat, Jordan has Paul traveling from city to city by bus.[51]

2) Use of Local Colloquialisms and Idioms

One of the most delightful aspects of Jordan's Cotton Patch version of the scriptures is the way in which he intersperses southern colloquialisms and expressions into his writing. He particularly uses this strategy when translating narrative passages in the Gospels and Acts.

From Matthew:

> When Jesus was born in Gainesville, Ga., during the time that Herod was governor, some scholars from the Orient came to Atlanta and inquired, "Where is the one who was born to be governor of Georgia? We saw his star in the Orient, and we came to honor him." This news put Governor Herod and all his Atlanta cronies in a tizzy. So he called a meeting of the big-time preachers and politicians and asked if they had any idea where the Leader was to be born.[52]

---

49. Jordan, *Luke and Acts*, 42–43.
50. Ibid., 78.
51. Jordan, *Luke and Acts*. See especially 141, his discussion of Acts 21:1ff.
52. Jordan, *Matthew and John*, 2–3.

After they had checked out, the Lord's messenger made connection with Joseph in a dream and said, "Get moving, and take your wife and baby and highball it to Mexico. Then stay put until I get word to you, because Herod is going to do his best to kill the baby."[53]

Come to me all you who are frustrated and have a bellyful, and I will give you zest. Get in the harness with me and let me teach you, for I am trained and have a cooperative spirit, and you will find zest for your lives. For my harness is practical and my assignment is joyful.[54]

From Luke:

When Simon (Rock) saw it all, he got down on his knees before Jesus and said, "Don't waste your time on a bum like me, sir!" For he and his buddies were bug-eyed because of the big wad of fish they had caught.[55]

When they heard [what Jesus said], the whole congregation blew a gasket.[56]

Word reached Governor Herod about all that was happening, and he was flabbergasted.[57]

A man throwing a dinner party said, "Ya'll come. It's all ready."[58]

One time in a certain city there was a judge who didn't believe in God, and who didn't give a hoot about people.[59]

Keep away from those religious leaders who insist on wearing academic robes and who love the back-slapping at the civic clubs and the center chairs in the pulpits and the speakers' tables at banquets; who eat widows out of house and home, and make long prayers at the drop of a hat. These will get the Judgement book thrown at them.[60]

From Acts:

53. Ibid., 3.
54. Jordan, *Matthew and John*, 25.
55. Jordan, *Luke and Acts*, 27.
56. Ibid., 27.
57. Ibid., 40–41.
58. Ibid., 59.
59. Ibid., 67.
60. Ibid., 76.

After the outpouring of the Holy Spirit on Pentecost: "Everybody was dumbfounded and puzzled, saying to one another, 'What's the meaning of this?' But others sneered, 'They're tanked up on white lightning.'"[61]

Now Governor Herod was having a knock-down, drag-out fight with the Education Commission and the Welfare Department.[62]

3) Translating Ancient Words, Images and Concepts Into Modern Ones

Another strategy Jordan uses to contemporize the scriptures is to translate the Bible's ancient words, images and concepts into modern, local, southern ones. For example: "This guy John was dressed in blue jeans and a leather jacket, and he was living on corn bread and collard greens. Folks were coming to him from Atlanta and all over north Georgia and the backwater of the Chattahoochee. And as they owned up to their crooked ways, he dipped them in the Chattahoochee."[63]

Jesus' instructions to the twelve disciples: "Take nothing on your trip—no sleeping bag, no suitcase, no bread, no money, not even two suits. When you are invited to a home, you may use it as a base of operations. If no one will invite you, leave that city without so much as a particle of dust from it clinging to your feet as evidence to them that you've taken nothing of theirs."[64]

The loaves and the fishes: "Between us there's no more than five boxes of crackers and two cans of sardines."[65]

"How terribly difficult it is for those who own things to come into the God Movement. Actually it's easier to thread a needle with a rope than for a rich man to get into the God Movement."[66]

Jordan also tries to simplify complex theological terms—again translating them into language that is more common in twentieth-century American. Instead of saying "the kingdom of God," he talks throughout his

---

61. Ibid., 93.
62. Ibid., 120.
63. Jordan, *Matthew and John* 5.
64. Jordan, *Luke and Acts*, 40.
65. Ibid., 41.
66. Ibid., 69.

Cotton Patch versions about "the God Movement." Instead of talking about Jesus as "the Son of God" he calls him "God's appointed leader."[67] He refers to Satan as "the Confuser."[68]

4) Use of Examples and Illustrations from Everyday Life

While the use of local idiom and speech is one aspect of preaching as "folk art," another is the use of examples and illustrations that are reflective of life as members of the congregation actually experience it. "Preaching as folk art looks for ways to enflesh the gospel in events and people and circumstances that are ordinary and commonplace to the hearers. Rather than aiming for the grandiose, the miraculous, and the extraordinary in illustrative materials, such preaching strives to enflesh the gospel in the real-life stories about real-life people in real-life situations with which a local congregation can identify."[69]

Once again, Jordan models the kind of proclamation I am talking about. When you read his published sermons, you do not find him using canned illustrations that do not have the ring of authenticity and truth about them. Nor do you find him holding up as models larger than life heroes like Mother Teresa or Martin Luther King, Jr. Instead, Jordan's sermons are peppered with stories from everyday life in southwest Georgia—including a number that reference his own experiences at Koinonia Farm.

For example, Jordan tells the following personal story to illustrate how the church that is the "womb" of our faith, can also turn on us if we are truly about God's business:

> The Church, in a very real sense gives birth to sons of God. She is the womb in which they are conceived. In my own case this was true. The little Baptist church in which I grew up nurtured me. In its womb I learned the Scriptures. I suckled at its breasts. And the little church thought that it was not only my mother, but also my father. And when I began to go about my Father's business, the Church said, "No, son, you're piercing our hearts. We don't want to give you up." And when I finally persisted in going about my Father's business, my mother, the Church, renounced me.[70]

---

67. Ibid., 42.
68. Jordan, Matthew and John, 6.
69. Tisdale, *Preaching as Local Theology*, 130.
70. Jordan, "The Womb of God," in *The Substance of Faith*, 12.

Jordan here is referencing the fact that the local Southern Baptist Church in Americus, Georgia disfellowshipped him and his family because of their stand on race. He uses that experience to illumine the way in which Mary, the mother of Jesus, had to relinquish Jesus and allow him to be about his Father's business.

In a sermon on Matthew 5, where Jesus tells us not to worry about our lives, Jordan tells a story about how, at the founding of Koinonia Farm, he and Martin England, Koinonia's co-founder, had no idea where they were going to get the $2500 down payment for the farm, but how God provided. He concludes his story in this manner:

> Years later, a newspaper reporter came out there and asked, "Who finances this project?"
> Well, all along, folks who had helped us said the Lord had sent them, so I said to this newspaper report, "The Lord does."
> "Yeah," he said. "I know. But who supports it?"
> I said, "The Lord."
> "Yeah, I know," he said, "but who, who, who, un, who—you know what I'm talking about? Who's back of it?"
> I said, "The Lord."
> He said, "But what I mean is, how do you pay your bills?"
> I said, "By check."
> "But," he said. "I mean—hell, don't you know what I mean?"
> I said, "Yeah, friend, I know what you mean. The trouble is you don't know what I mean."[71]

And in a sermon preached on Ephesians 5, as an illustration of how hard it can be to follow in Christ's way, Jordan tells a very poignant story about how his daughter Jan ended up sitting in the bleachers at her own high school graduation, rather than graduating with the rest of her class, because a Negro friend of hers was denied admittance to the ceremonies. Jordan comments: "An honors student made a speech on moral responsibility and another student made a speech on reverence for God and man, and Jan was sitting up there in the stands in her cap and gown. Her name was never called. She never received her diploma. She was a pilgrim, a sojourner, and I must confess, that night with her white cap and gown on I was real proud of her. She looked like an angel sojourner to me. She was feeling the sting of the pilgrimage, of being a sojourner in a strange land."[72]

---

71. Jordan, "Was Jesus Really Poor?," in *The Substance of Faith*, 91.
72. Jordan, "Jesus Christ Revealed," in *The Substance of Faith*, 111.

But not all of Jordan's examples are personal or Koinonia-based. As a way of illustrating the fact that we in the church prefer that God remain God and not become a real live human being, Jordan tells this story:

> A church in Georgia just set up a big twenty-five-thousand-dollar granite fountain on its lawn, circulating water to the tune of one thousand gallons a minute. Now that ought to be enough to satisfy any Baptist. But what on earth is a church doing taking God Almighty's money in a time of great need like this and setting up a little old fountain on its lawn to bubble water around? *I was thirsty . . . and ye built me a fountain.* We can handle God as long as he stays God. We can build him a fountain. But when he becomes a man we have to give him a cup of water. So the virgin birth is simply the great transcendent truth that God Almighty has come into the affairs of man and dwells among us.[73]

And to illustrate the fact that it's easier to reshape the gospel to conform to our lives than it is to reshape our lives in conformity with the gospel, Jordan uses this illustration:

> I just got a real beautiful, slick advertisement in the mail a while back. It's put out by a publishing company of religious books and records. It says, "This is your personal invitation to set sail on a Christian voyage of self-discovery in the company of three great Christian leaders." And when you open it up, you find that you can get an inside berth for three hundred sixty dollars that week. But that's where the poor folks sleep. The really elite who are going to discover themselves sleep on the A deck in a deluxe outside room at six hundred thirty dollars for the week.
> . . . Where can you find a better place to find Christ than in the congenial, comfortable atmosphere of an ocean liner? That's easy to answer—anywhere. If these people want to know where to make a self-discovery, let them walk down the streets of Calcutta. Let them go to the market in Kinshasa. Let them go to Accra, Ghana. Let them go to any ghetto in America or any little country shack in rural America.[74]

Often Jordan's preaching does not need examples or illustrations because of the way in which he collapses the distance between the biblical world and the contemporary world, allowing his hearers to actually become participants in the biblical story themselves. But when he does use them, his

---

73. Jordan, "The Sons of God," in *The Substance of Faith*, 15.
74. Jordan, "The Humanity of God," in *The Substance of Faith*, 27.

stories and illustrations serve to enhance the folk artistry of his preaching—bringing it even closer to the soil of his southwest Georgia listeners.

Conclusion

As anyone reading this can readily tell, I am a big fan of Clarence Jordan and his preaching. Although I never personally had opportunity to meet him, I feel like I know the man through his writings and his life's witness. I deeply admire the way in which he courageously proclaimed and incarnated the prophetic gospel of Christ in both word and deed. And I frequently use his sermons and Cotton Patch translations as classroom examples of contextual preaching and prophetic preaching at their best.

This is not to say, however, that Jordan was without flaws. Some of his views on women are troubling—especially given the times in which he was writing. In one sermon he actually defends Paul's injunction that men should be heads of the household and that women should be subservient to them.[75] He also buys into the belief (common at the time) that homosexuality is a sin and at one juncture includes "homos" in a long list of people who are disobedient to God. But it is also the case that even these inconsistencies in his thinking stand out all the more because Jordan is so very consistent otherwise. At heart he has a passion for justice, equality, and peace that are as admirable today as they were half a century ago. And his preaching has much to teach us about how we might more effectively proclaim the whole prophetic gospel of God in our own day and time.

---

75. In his sermon, "Making a Habit of Love," Jordan says: "You [ladies] may not believe that the man is head of the woman, but perhaps it's true right on. It has been my experience in what little bit of marriage counseling I've done that one of the major causes of difficulty in the home is that the husband and wife get confused as to what their role is. Much of the difficulty in the home arises from the fact that woman wants to be the man and the man is weak enough to let her." *The Substance of Faith*, 126.

2

The Cotton Patch Versions

Why Do We Love Them So Much?

Ann Coble

I have given many talks about Clarence Jordan and his work at Koinonia Farm. The audiences have been academics, church leaders, and what Clarence would call "plain church folk." One thing I have noticed is that everyone loves the unusual and special paraphrases we call the Cotton Patch versions. Why? What is so attractive about these versions of some of the New Testament books? What draws in Catholics and Mennonites, Southerners and Northerners, adults and children, almost everyone so that they are gripped by these translations? There are probably a number of answers to this question, but I am going to focus on three.

First, the way the Cotton Patch versions came into being was spontaneous and organic. Because of this, they do not seem forced or overly planned out. They feel authentic. To help you see this, let me explain how the Cotton Patch versions came into being.

In addition to the work on the farm, Clarence would travel around preaching and teaching at churches, college fellowships, and retreats. As many of you know, he had a PhD in Greek New Testament. He would preach using only a few notes and his Greek Bible, translating into the Georgia dialect as he went. As early as 1955, Clarence's supporters were asking him to write down his own personal translations of the New Testament. After hearing about Rock and Andy Johnson and Mary and Joe Davidson in his sermons, people wanted to see what Clarence's version would look like in a written translation. Russ Berry, a college Sunday school teacher at Grant Park Baptist Church in Portland, Oregon, asked Clarence, "Have you done a complete translation of the entire New Testament? If so, is it available?"[1]

Clarence's version of sections of the New Testament became better known as he preached around the country, and not just among church groups. In the spring of 1960, James S. Best of the Associated Press contacted Clarence about writing "a book on the Greek Testament translated freely for today."[2]

Clarence decided to create what he called "cotton patch" versions of the books of the New Testament. With Clarence's emphasis on Jesus and the Sermon on the Mount, one might expect that he would begin with Matthew or at least one of the Gospels, but Clarence began with Hebrews and James.[3] This makes sense because Clarence was writing these for a primarily Christian audience. He wanted to find biblical texts that pushed his readers to act, to be involved, and to do good works. Hebrews, with its emphasis on running the race to the end, and James, with its slogan that faith without works is dead, were just what Clarence was looking for.[4] There were plenty of people in his audiences and also in his neighborhood who would claim to be Christians, but Clarence wanted to challenge these people to act like they really believed.

In the Translator's Notes to Hebrews and the general epistles, Clarence gives his reason for choosing these texts. He said these writings "come from some of the earliest partners in the faith of Jesus Christ and sparkle with keen insight and spiritual perception."[5] Clarence liked the fact that

---

1. Letter from Russ Berry to Clarence Jordan, Clarence Jordan Papers, Hargrett Rare Book and Manuscript Library at the University of Georgia Libraries, Athens, Georgia, Manuscript #756, Box 3, Folder 3, May 16, 1955.

2. Letter from James S. Best to Clarence Jordan, Clarence Jordan Papers, Hargrett Rare Book and Manuscript Library at the University of Georgia Libraries, Athens, Georgia, Manuscript #756, Box 6, Folder 1, May 13, 1960.

3. Clarence Jordan, *The Cotton Patch Version of Hebrews and the General Epistles* (Clinton, NJ: New Win, 1973), 6; the Cotton Patch version of Hebrews was first copyrighted in 1963 and James was copyrighted in 1964.

4. Hebrews 12:1–2 and James 2:26.

5. Jordan, *The Cotton Patch Version of Hebrews and the General Epistles*, 15.

these letters "abound in compassion, love, encouragement, and hope."[6] He wanted his readers to be gripped with a passion for living out their faith, and he thought these letters would provide the "fiery zeal" which would warn them of "the perils of indifference and lukewarmness."[7] Clarence hoped that these modern paraphrases would bring these biblical texts into the twentieth century in such a way as to incite people to action.

Although later Cotton Patch versions became well known because of the views on race that were included, these first translations were a simpler attempt to update the texts. In many ways they were very similar to the paraphrase *The Message*,[8] but slightly more Southern-sounding. In later works, Clarence translated the tension between Jews and Gentiles into the tension between blacks and whites. The setting is actually in Georgia, and he used names of Georgia cities. However, in these early translations, he retained the biblical place names of Jerusalem, Mount Sinai, and Egypt, and he kept the Jew/Gentile distinction. Sometimes, but not consistently, Jewish leaders are translated as clergymen.[9] In many ways, these early Cotton Patch versions were as tied to the first century as to the twentieth. What made them unique was the use of South Georgia language. Here is an example from Hebrews 12:1–3: "Now here's where we come in. Surrounded by such a cloud of veterans of the faith, let's strip off all heavy and tight-fitting clothes and run with endurance the race stretching out before us. Let's keep our eyes fixed on Jesus, the founder and guiding spirit of our way of life. In place of joy that stretched out before him, he took on a cross, without hesitating one second to consider the disgrace involved."[10]

When Clarence translated James, he began to include some of his ideas about racial reconciliation, although only to a small degree. James 2:8 is an example of how Clarence began incorporating ideas about race into his translations: "So if you observe the Scripture's finest law—'Love your neighbor as yourself'—you're doing all right. But if you segregate, you commit a sin, and stand convicted under the law as a violator."[11]

---

6. Ibid.

7. Jordan, *The Cotton Patch Version of Hebrews and the General Epistles*, 15.

8. Eugene H. Peterson, *The Message: The Bible in Contemporary Language* (Colorado Springs: NavPress, 2005).

9. Jordan, *The Cotton Patch Version of Hebrews and the General Epistles*, 28–30.

10. Ibid., 38–39.

11. Ibid., 49.

One of the most well known phrases from the Cotton Patch versions comes from Clarence's translation of Hebrews 11:1: "Now faith is the turning of dreams into deeds; it is betting your life on the unseen realities."[12] This phrase "turning dreams into deeds" became even more well-known when Henlee Barnette used it as the subtitle to his book on Clarence's ethics.[13] Clarence had made the Bible clearer for the lay people in his community and in the churches where he preached, but his later versions are much more radical, and therefore more controversial.

After Jordan translated the letters attributed to Paul, he realized he wanted to write a defense of his version, which he included in the preface to *The Cotton Patch Version of Paul's Epistles*.[14] In translating these texts, he had taken a more revolutionary approach to translating. He was now making a stronger statement against racism and he was bringing the texts closer to the twentieth century. Clarence lists three intentions of this new style of translating, the first being the problem of cultural distance. He complains that modern translations "still have left us stranded in some faraway land in the long-distant past."[15] Calling these projects versions rather than translations, he said he wanted people to be participants in the Christian faith, and he did this by translating "not only the words but the events."[16] Clarence wanted the words to be alive and relevant for twentieth-century America.

Clarence said he wanted the scriptures to be "taken out of the classroom and stained-glass sanctuary and put out under God's skies where people are toiling and crying and wondering."[17] He did not want the letters of Paul to become formal or academic, but to be seen as letters written to simple, humble people.[18] He wanted the "little people of great faith" whom he found in rural church pews and out working in their fields to understand Jesus' message in their own words.[19]

---

12. Ibid., 35.

13. Henlee Barnette, *Clarence Jordan: Turning Dreams Into Deeds* (Macon, GA: Smith and Helwys, 1992).

14. Clarence Jordan, *The Cotton Patch Version of Paul's Epistles* (Clinton, NJ: New Win, 1968), 7–11.

15. Ibid., 7.

16. Ibid.

17. Ibid.

18. See Jordan, *The Cotton Patch Version of Paul's Epistles*, 11 for a discussion of Pauline authorship.

19. Ibid., 8.

Clarence then described his theory of translation in more detail. He stated that he was trying to translate the ideas, not the words. He was concerned that often the "actual words convey the wrong impression to the modern hearer."[20] Given that he was working not only with two languages that were separated by a huge time gap, but also "the barriers of culture and space," Clarence admitted that it was hard to find present-day equivalents.[21] For example, Clarence translated the word *crucifixion* as lynching. He thought the ideas of violence, indignity, stigma, and defeat were best conveyed to a Southern audience by the term *lynching*, but he admitted that lynchings lacked the trial and legal condemnation that characterized Jesus' crucifixion.[22] By the time he was translating the Gospels, his versions were a natural, organic outgrowth of his own cultural and religious setting. We hear that naturalness, that authentic voice when we read these versions.

Secondly, we love these versions because Clarence made his translations fun and funny. His versions of the Gospels are particularly enjoyable. Sometimes they are laugh-out-loud hilarious and sometimes they are extremely quick-witted. It brings a smile to imagine this version of the story of John the Baptist:

> Now during the fifteenth year of Tiberius as President, while Pontius Pilate was governor of Georgia, and Herod was governor of Alabama, his brother Philip being governor of Mississippi, and Lysanias still holding out over Arkansas; while Annas and Caiaphas were co-presidents of the Southern Baptist Convention, the word of God came to Zack's boy, John, down on the farm.
>
> This guy John was dressed in blue jeans and a leather jacket, and he was living on corn bread and collard greens. Folks were coming to him from Atlanta and all over north Georgia and the backwater of the Chattahoochee. And as they owned up to their crooked ways, he dipped them in the Chattahoochee.[23]

Jesus was born in Gainsville and laid in an apple box. When Herod, who was governor of Georgia, hears that a new governor was prophesied by the wise men, "this news put Governor Herod and all his Atlanta cronies

20. Ibid., 9.
21. Ibid., 8.
22. Ibid., 8–9.
23. Jordan, Clarence. *The Cotton Patch Version of Matthew and John* (Clinton, NJ: New Win, 1970), 18, and Jordan, *The Cotton Patch Version of Luke and Acts* (Clinton, NJ; New Win, 1969), 21.

in a tizzy."[24] Rather than fleeing to Egypt, Joseph is told to take his family and "highball it to Mexico."[25] The religious center is Atlanta.[26] That terrible, awful city that has Judea under its thumb is Washington, D.C.—quite a humorous thought for a Southerner.[27] Part of the enjoyment of reading these versions is in seeing how cleverly Jordan translated these familiar texts. The reason the Cotton Patch play and musical, which Clarence did not write but that were based on his Cotton Patch versions, work so well is that they are downright funny!

Thirdly, we are drawn to these versions not only because they make us laugh but because they make us cry. They stab us in heart. We are cut to the quick. This is particularly evident when it comes to seeing the Gospels in light of racial tensions. Perhaps the most important decision that Clarence made in his Cotton Patch versions was to translate Jew and Gentile (and Pharisee and sinner) as "white man and Negro."[28] In considering this decision, Clarence asked, "In the Southern context, is there any other alternative?"[29] The good Samaritan has become an often-quoted parable because it hits at the heart of racism. I am rendering Clarence's footnotes as part of the text.

> One day a teacher of an adult Bible class got up and tested him with this question: "Doctor, what does one do to be saved?"
>
> Jesus replied, "What does the Bible say? How do you interpret it?"
>
> The teacher answered, "Love the Lord your God with all your heart and with all your soul and with all your physical strength and with all your mind; and love your neighbor as yourself."
>
> "That is correct," answered Jesus. "Make a habit of this and you'll be saved."
>
> But the Sunday school teacher, trying to save face, asked, "But ... er ... but ... just who *is* my neighbor?"
>
> Then Jesus laid into him and said, "A man was going from Atlanta to Albany and some gangsters held him up. When they had robbed him of his wallet and brand-new suit, they beat him up

---

24. Jordan, *The Cotton Patch Version of Matthew and John*, 16.
25. Ibid., 17.
26. Jordan, *The Cotton Patch Version of Matthew and John*, 16–17; and Jordan, *The Cotton Patch Version of Luke and Acts*, 18–20.
27. Jordan, *The Cotton Patch Version of Paul's Epistles*, 15ff.
28. Ibid., 9.
29. Ibid.

and drove off in his car, leaving him unconscious on the shoulder of the highway.

"Now it just so happened that a white preacher was going down that same highway. When he saw the fellow, he stepped on the gas and went scooting by. (His homiletical mind probably made the following outline: 1. I do not know the man. 2. I do not wish to get involved in any court proceedings. 3. I don't want to get blood on my new upholstering. 4. The man's lack of proper clothing would embarrass me upon my arrival in town. 5. And finally, brethren, a minister must never be late for worship services.)[30]

"Shortly afterwards a white Gospel song leader came down the road, and when he saw what had happened, he too stepped on the gas. (What his thoughts were we'll never know, but as he whizzed past, he may have been whistling, 'Brighten the corner, where you are.')[31]

"Then a black man traveling that way came upon the fellow, and what he saw moved him to tears. He stopped and bound up his wounds as best he could, drew some water from his water-jug to wipe away the blood and then laid him on the back seat. (All the while his thoughts may have been along this line: 'Somebody's robbed you; yeah, I know about that, I been robbed, too. And they done beat you up bad; I know, I been beat up, too. And everybody just go right on by and leave you laying there hurting. Yeah, I know. They pass me by, too.')[32] He drove into Albany and took him to the hospital and said to the nurse, 'You all take good care of this white man I found on the highway. Here's the only two dollars I got, but you all keep account of what he owes, and if he can't pay it, I'll settle up with you when I make a pay-day.'

"Now if you had been the man held up by the gangsters, which of these three—the white preacher, the white song leader, or the black man—would you consider to have been the neighbor?"

The teacher of the adult Bible class said, "Why, of course, the nig - I mean, er . . . well, er . . . the one who treated me kindly."

Jesus said, "Well, then *you* get going and start living like that!"[33]

It is obvious that, as stated above, Clarence has set the scene so that racist white people are equated with the Pharisees and Jewish leaders who

---

30. Jordan's original footnote, *The Cotton Patch Version of Luke and Acts*, 47 n. 7.
31. Ibid., footnote 8.
32. Ibid., footnote 9.
33. Jordan, *The Cotton Patch Version of Luke and Acts*, 46–47, Luke 10:25–37, Jordan's italics.

rejected Jesus, and the African Americans and sympathetic white people are equated with the Gentiles and sinners and the Jews who followed Jesus. It is no wonder Clarence irritated local church people. It could hardly be any clearer—for Clarence, it was the white church people and Sunday school teachers who were against Jesus.

Conclusion

While I am sure there are many more reasons why we may love the Cotton Patch versions, I have chosen to highlight these three: the authenticity that comes from the natural birth of these translations, the humor that is woven through most of them (especially the Gospels), and the power that comes from the truth of the cultural critiques. We laugh, we cry, and we are gripped to our very core.

Perhaps the crowd's response to Jesus' words in the Sermon on the Mount is also applicable to our responses to Clarence's Cotton Patch versions: "The people were simply amazed at his ideas, for he was teaching them like he knew what he was talking about. He didn't sound like *their* preachers."[34]

---

34. Jordan, *The Cotton Patch Version of Matthew and John,* 31, Matthew 7:28–29, Jordan's italics.

PART TWO

Grace and Healing

3

Clarence Jordan as a (White) Interpreter of the Bible

Greg Carey

Clarence Jordan has drawn widely divergent reviews as a biblical interpreter. In his own day some Bible professors derided Jordan as a poor exegete, presumably because he understood key passages in Acts to teach absolute relinquishment of property rather than occasional, habitual sharing.[1] In pastoral theology we might call this the "presenting issue," the complaint people voice when they're not prepared to name the fundamental, underlying problem. I disagree with Jordan's interpretation of those Acts passages, as do most interpreters, but I suspect the criticism had more to do with Jordan's discipleship than with his exegetical skills.

Others, not least the great Baptist ethicists Henlee Barnette and James McClendon, acknowledge Jordan's doctoral work in Greek New Testament but tend to emphasize the simplicity of his approach to Scripture.[2] One

---

1. Will D. Campbell, "Where There's So Much Smoke: Thirty-Caliber Violence at Koinonia," *Sojourners* 8 (Dec 1979), excerpted online at http://www.koinoniapartners.org/History/Violence.html.

2. Henlee H. Barnette, Henlee H. *Clarence Jordan: Turning Dreams into Deeds* (Macon, GA: Smith & Helwys, 1992), 13–14, citing James McClendon, *Biography as Theology* (Nashville: Abingdon, 1974), 117.

Southern Baptist missions executive recalled Jordan as a "starry-eyed idealist" with "simplistic, naive New Testament principles."[3] Such accounts essentially portray Jordan as a naïve biblicist who happened to know Greek very, very well. Citing Barnette, Ann Louise Coble describes his approach to the Bible as "more conservative" than that of his professors.[4] For his part, Barnette estimates Jordan's sophistication more highly than does McClendon: "While literary and form criticism were not stressed by [Jordan's] professors, Clarence was introduced to the critical method in his advanced courses in New Testament. While he may not have gained much knowledge about ethical and social issues from his teachers, he learned a lot about Koine Greek."[5] In Barnette's assessment neither Jordan's Southern Baptist upbringing nor his theological education at Southern Baptist Theological Seminary provided a theological framework for engaging the pressing, even crushing, social issues of the time.

Far be it from me to quarrel with Henlee Barnette, who represented a guiding light in my own struggles to claim a livable Southern Baptist heritage and in whose classroom I once enjoyed the privilege of studying. I recall walking across the Southern Seminary campus, on my way to Barnette's ministerial ethics class, and reflecting, "I bet Clarence Jordan made this same walk." Barnette knew Jordan intimately, and he knew Southern Baptist life, particularly the idiosyncrasies of Southern Seminary, as well as anyone could. He knew the times and the cultural norms in ways that are lost to me. So rather than quarrel, I will humbly demur.

For example, P. Joel Snider sketches quite a different picture. Snider points out how Jordan's excellent academic performance led to a series of job offers, including an academic post at Tift College. Jordan also cultivated relationships with Baptists at a national level, speaking to national gatherings at the Ridgecrest Baptist Assembly, writing for Woman's Missionary Union publications, and speaking on campuses such as Baylor and Furman.[6] Snider draws upon others who described Jordan as being "as much

---

3. Letter from H. Cornell Goerner, in Barnette, *Clarence Jordan*, 93.

4. Ann Louise Coble, *Cotton Patch for the Kingdom: Clarence Jordan's Demonstration Plot at Koinonia Farm* (Scottdale, PA: Herald Press, 2001), 40.

5. Barnette, *Clarence Jordan*, 14. Relying on Barnette, Coble characterizes Jordan's professors as moderates who taught the critical method (*Cotton Patch for the Kingdom*, 40).

6. P. Joel Snider, *The "Cotton Patch" Gospel: The Proclamation of Clarence Jordan* (Lanham, MD: University Press of America, 1985), 12–13. For Baylor, see David Stricklin, *A Genealogy of Dissent: Southern Baptist Protest in the Twentieth Century* (Lexington: University of Kentucky Press, 1999), 66.

at home in a hay field as on a lecture podium" and possessing a "rare combination of Greek scholarship and the practical imagery of a dirt farmer."[7] One hardly gets the impression of a naïve, albeit intelligent, country boy with an intense passion for the gospel.

Then again, we might seek the assessment of one particularly informed observer, Clarence Jordan himself. Unfortunately for this project, Jordan excelled in two distinctively Southern skills that raise problems for the historian. A smart Southerner routinely deflects praise from himself or herself, sometimes to the point of tedium. A wily Southerner furthermore possesses the subtle skill of informing people just who the hell they are dealing with without coming across as bragging. Jordan practiced both skills with admirable competence.

On the one hand, Jordan deemphasizes his intellectual qualifications. He occasionally calls himself a fundamentalist.[8] He routinely pokes fun at professors and their institutions, referring to his seminary as the "cemetery."[9] In response to the invitation to provide Southern Seminary's then prestigious Gheens Lectures, Jordan assessed the opportunity as "mighty fine cotton for a pea-picking farmer like me."[10]

On the other hand, at some moments Jordan gives away the extent of his learning. He refuses to be liberal or conservative, though his opinions clearly place him in conversation with liberal theology and ethics.[11] His sermons are full of little lectures on history, tidbits of Greek grammar, and vocabulary. He alludes to scholarly opinion and even to the consensus opinions of scholars.[12] Jordan attributes his advanced study of Greek to his desire for intellectual integrity, even superiority, in arguments that would take place in the Jim Crow South.[13] Rigorous thinking was important to Jordan; he simply didn't want to dress it up in such a way as to alienate his audience.

---

7. Snider, "Cotton Patch" Gospel, 3.

8. As in *The Substance of Faith and Other Cotton Patch Sermons*, ed. Dallas Lee (New York: Association Press, 1972), 30.

9. Jordan, *The Substance of Faith*, 32.

10. Barnette, *Clarence Jordan*, 8.

11. As in *Substance of Faith*, 17, 46.

12. He discusses scholarly dismissal of Paul's authorship of Ephesians (*The Cotton Patch Version of Paul's Epistles* [New York: Association Press, 1968], 11), Peter's authorship of 1 Peter (*Substance of Faith*, 98), and the second century date of Daniel (46–47).

13. Jordan, *The Substance of Faith*, 108.

I am a New Testament scholar, and my focus will rest on Clarence Jordan's work as a biblical interpreter. I am not a Jordan biographer, nor a cultural historian, nor a theologian. I know just a bit about activism among Southern Christians in the middle of the twentieth century, all from reading the work of historians, and I know a good deal about the history of biblical scholarship and its responses to the theological movements of the past two centuries. Clarence Jordan was a white Southerner who carried out public biblical interpretation. In the context of his times I suspect that his interpretive work was perhaps more sophisticated than many recognize.

Context

When I introduce Clarence Jordan in churches and classrooms, I often begin, "Clarence Jordan founded a racially integrated farming community in Georgia in 1942. In *Georgia*. In *1942*." I'm hoping the allusions to place and time invite a sense of wonder at Jordan's prophetic heroism. And yes, many of us treat Jordan as a hero, a man who stood out starkly in his own place and time, a man rejected by his alma mater, by his church, and by white society in general.

All that is true, of course, but we also recall that Jordan called Koinonia "a demonstration plot for the kingdom of God," and he also called the kingdom "the God movement." In other words, Jordan wanted to participate in a movement, not live as a solitary hero. And so he did. In his seminary days Jordan found about another dozen students who were willing to pool their resources and engage in boundary crossing ministry. He found partners to initiate Koinonia, just as he found partners for the Fund for Humanity, from which we now have both the Fuller Center for Housing and Habitat for Humanity.

Not only did Jordan labor in community, in many ways he was a person of his times. The general theological climate of Jordan's day suggests that Jordan's thinking did not form in the sort of isolation suggested by Barnette. Though Southern Seminary was hardly a hotbed for social radicalism, some faculty members did express progressive sentiments. One, Edward A. McDowell, Jr., took Jordan along to a Southern Interracial Committee meeting.[14] Moreover, Louisville already provided a nexus for South-

---

14. Tracy Elaine K'Meyer, *Interracialism and Christian Community in the Postwar South: The Story of Koinonia Farm* (Charlottesville: University of Virginia Press, 1997), 29; Charles Marsh, *The Beloved Community: How Faith Shapes Social Justice, from the Civil Rights Movement to Today* (New York: Basic Books, 2005), 63.

ern Baptist social ministry prior to Clarence Jordan's arrival. Louisville was home to the Woman's Missionary Union Training School for Christian Workers. This school later merged in 1963 with Southern Seminary, eventually to become the Carver School of Church Social Work.[15] That Jordan fielded so many speaking invitations and job offers during his seminary career reveals that he did not pursue his interests in isolation.

The quietism that may have marked some of Jordan's theological education does not exhaust the range of influences that nourished him. Charles Marsh locates Jordan within "a period of innovation in race relations among Southern Baptist progressives."[16] Indeed, the era in which Jordan studied theology, practiced what we now call social ministry, and initiated the Koinonia project stands out for a peculiar stream of white Christian activism in the South. I do not mean to credit Christianity for all the activism of the period, nor would I overestimate the influence and success of the movement, but Clarence Jordan knew and corresponded with folks like Myles Horton, founder of what is now the Highlander Center, and Howard Kester, a labor organizer and onetime executive secretary of the Fellowship of Southern Churchmen.[17] People like Horton and Kester experienced their own theological formation in the legacy of the social gospel an in conversation with influential faculty members at the Union Theological Seminary in New York City and the School of Religion at Vanderbilt University.

The social gospel movement emerged in the late nineteenth century. It emphasized Jesus' practical work to improve people's lives, and it sought the kingdom of God in terms of a society that attains dignity and equity for all its members. The irrational slaughter of the First World War, followed by the devastation of the Great Depression, required a more measured, more critical assessment of the notion of "progress," and theologians like Union Seminary's Reinhold Niebuhr responded with a critique of social gospel optimism, complemented by stronger interpretations of sin and its

---

15. Southern Seminary transferred ownership of the Carver School to Campbellsville University in 1998.

16. Marsh, *The Beloved Community*, 63.

17. Marsh summarizes Jordan's interaction with Kester in an extensive footnote (*Beloved Community*, 238–39, n. 44). See also Andrew S. Chancey, "Race, Religion, and Agricultural Reform: The Communal Vision of Koinonia Farm," in *Georgia in Black and White: Explorations in Race Relations of a Southern State, 1865–1950*, ed. John C. Inscoe (Athens, GA: University of Georgia Press, 2010), 250. The classic study of Southern radicalism remains Anthony P. Dunbar, *Against the Grain: Southern Radicals and Prophets, 1929–1959* (Charlottesville: University Press of Virginia, 1981); see Stricklin, *A Genealogy of Dissent*.

pervasiveness. During Jordan's Louisville years Henlee Barnette himself had turned to Walter Rauschenbusch, a founding theologian of the social gospel, and the more contemporary Niebuhr for guidance—where did he get that idea if not through his studies at Southern?[18] For his part, Clarence Jordan had little patience for empty liberal optimism. Nevertheless, his emphasis upon incarnational ministry and the kingdom of God as a present social reality reflects the influence of social gospel teaching upon his imagination.

We can only imagine Jordan's personal journey in the area of race relations. The hero's coming to racial awareness amounts to a required topos of Southern liberal hagiography, and Jordan devotees know one story from his childhood. Jordan's tale, of hearing the groaning of a tortured prisoner and knowing that just hours before the warden who was supervising the torture had been praising God in church, is compelling enough. But such singular memories often represent a longer, more indirect process—and that is the case with Jordan.[19] Yet other Southern liberals recount their own struggles in coming to terms with genuine equality. Though disposed to help African Americans, they found themselves unprepared for genuine social interaction. Some reported being unable to swallow during common meals or being unable to sleep when circumstances required mixed bunking.[20] We do not know, or at least I do not know, how Jordan moved from a passion for justice to his ability to transgress such obstacles even during his Louisville days.

Clarence Jordan was no solitary hero. He was not the only seminary educated white preacher, not the only white preacher, not the only white person to be concerned with racial and social justice. He sought community and fostered community well before his return to Georgia. He was in contact with teachers and colleagues who lived out the social gospel through sometimes risky activism. He learned from his African American students at Simmons University, and he learned from the poor people among whom he ministered.[21] No more than Elvis invented rock and roll, Clarence Jordan did not invent the connection between the parable of the

---

18. Barnette, *Clarence Jordan*, 4. Barnette's 1948 Southern Seminary dissertation is "The Ethical Thought of Walter Rauschenbusch: A Critical Interpretation."

19. Marsh recounts several additional stories (*Beloved Community*, 58), citing Dallas Lee, *Cotton Patch Evidence* (New York: Harper & Row, 1971), 6.

20. Anecdotes from Dunbar, *Against the Grain*, 25, 33.

21. K'Meyer, *Interracialism and Christian Community*, 33–34.

Good Samaritan and the race problem. Hardly naïve, more theologically sophisticated and worldly than we might assume, Clarence Jordan was a person of his times and of a movement.

Jordan as Interpreter

The impression of Clarence Jordan as a simplistic biblicist derives in part from Jordan's own self-presentation. Moreover, an initial encounter with Jordan through the *Cotton Patch* translations and through his understanding of Acts 2 and 4 might lend itself to the same impression. *Cotton Patch* references to the "government," with a president and a governor and Southern Baptist officials headquartered in Atlanta, suggest a kind of naïve allegorization. No one seriously talks about the Roman "government" in the sense that we think of modern governments, while seminary students quickly learn that the Jerusalem temple was not simply a big church or denominational headquarters. Few contemporary interpreters would agree with Jordan's assessment that the Jerusalem church participated in a thorough communitarianism of the sort practiced at Koinonia.

But more is going on in Jordan's biblical interpretation than initially meets the eye. First of all, as a student of Greek Jordan well understood the complications and implications of translation. References to translation decisions and faulty renderings abound in Jordan's sermons and other writings. His introduction to the *Cotton Patch Version of Paul's Epistles* reflects his critical self-awareness, even confessing to the "unforgiveable sin of a self-respecting translator" by "self-imposing my own personal feelings."[22] He assumes his translations come across as "strained, crude, and perhaps even inaccurate."[23] Without using technical terminology, Jordan locates himself in the camp of dynamic equivalence translation that was just coming into vogue: he is translating not Paul's words but his ideas.[24]

In other words Jordan understood that translation isn't a simple mathematical equation. Translation requires overdetermination; that is, even when the translators themselves know that a text is ambiguous by design, translators have no choice but to interpret such passages for their readers. The best they can do is to supply the alternatives in a footnote.

---

22. Jordan, *Cotton Patch Version of Paul's Epistles*, 9.
23. Ibid., 8.
24. Ibid., 9.

Or maybe they can do better than that. Let's consider John 1:5. John's Gospel is notorious for its verbal ambiguity: does one need to be born "from above" or born "again" (John 3:3)? (Jordan chooses "from above.") Does Jesus say the wind blows where it chooses, or does he mean the Spirit does so (3:8)? (Jordan begins with "wind," then translates Jesus teaching concerning the "Spirit.") The New Revised Standard Version renders John 1:5 this way, without a footnote: "The light shines in the darkness, and the darkness did not *overcome* it." But according to the New American Standard Bible, "the darkness did not *comprehend*" the light. Which is it, overcome or comprehend?

Every intermediate Greek student knows the answer: this is a case of Johannine ambiguity. Two readings are possible, though one may be preferred. But Clarence Jordan outsmarted the translation committees: *And the light shines on in the darkness, and the darkness never quenched it.* "Quenched" is a perfect translation for *katalambanō*, the meaning of which can range from hostile conquest to the sort of conquest reflected in the attainment of understanding. Hostile or otherwise, darkness could not "quench" the light.

So Jordan demonstrated more sophistication and self-awareness as a translator than some might have thought.[25] We might reduce this reality to a matter of technical competence, if Jordan did not demonstrate hermeneutical sophistication in other aspects of his biblical interpretation. However, many of Jordan's signature interpretive moves reflect not solitary genius but his participation in a wider net of conversations.

By all accounts the kingdom of God figures prominently in Jordan's teaching. He famously translated the vexing term as "God movement," a decision that opens some possibilities while closing others. I assume that Jordan is undermining the too-popular association of "kingdom" with an institution and with a particular kind of coercive power. In contrast, "God movement" conveys the dynamic sense of Jesus' ministry and activities. But the word we translate as "kingdom," *basileia*, basically means "empire." Jesus' proclamation of the kingdom carried stronger anti-Roman resonances than "God movement" conveys. Jordan's translation gains the sense of Jesus' populist activism but obscures Jesus' critique of the Empire.

---

25. I should acknowledge that Jordan tended to make too much of etymology, breaking down words into their constituent parts and historical usage. James Barr's *The Semantics of Biblical Language* (Oxford: Oxford University Press, 1961), first published in 1961, effectively put an end to that practice.

A second rationale for Jordan's "God movement" rendering, however, clarifies Jordan's priorities. Some Gospel texts suggest "kingdom of God" as a future reality, something for which believers wait, while others indicate a present reality in which people participate. Jordan emphasized the kingdom of God's present reality. He outright rejected both individualistic and futuristic understandings of the kingdom, which equate the kingdom with the future eternal salvation of individual souls. "God movement" communicates the sense of communal participation that marked the Jesus movement.

Jordan's emphasis on what we might call "present eschatology," the realization of God's reign in the present, reflects both the social gospel's influence and a modernist sensibility concerning biblical language. Jordan was perfectly comfortable interpreting biblical stories as what he called "parables" rather than as historical realities. Daniel's friends are not actual persons who survived the fiery furnace,[26] and Jordan suspected that Joseph was indeed Jesus' biological father.[27] When it comes to eschatology, Christianity's ultimate hope, Jordan joined the social gospelers by looking to the here and now rather than to the by and by.[28] Jesus' resurrection, he argued, had more to do with Jesus' ongoing life in the church than to his translation to an ethereal spiritual realm.[29] Thus, the translation "God movement" strongly discourages pie in the sky futuristic speculation. Such teaching hardly suggests naïve biblicism.

We could multiply examples of Jordan's self-awareness as an interpreter. In some instances he demonstrates devotion to the principle that each Gospel speaks with its own distinctive voice and that interpreters ought not cram the Gospels' content into a blender. We see this when Jordan walks his audience through the twin narratives of Luke and Acts with scarcely a reference to other Gospels.[30] Yet when it suits him Jordan complements his narratives by mixing Gospel accounts, as when he appeals to John's prologue in interpreting Luke's account of Jesus' birth.[31] Although Jordan's dogged devotion to Jesus' teaching lends itself to the impression that he viewed the Gospels as transparent windows into the career and teaching of Jesus,

26. Jordan, *Substance of Faith*, 47.
27. Ibid., 19.
28. Ibid., 151.
29. Ibid., 14–19.
30. Ibid., 12–30.
31. Ibid., 25.

he also ventured idiosyncratic theories concerning inaccuracies in John's account of Judas.[32] Such examples suggest an interpreter whose violations of standard exegetical practice were intentional rather than naïve.

To this point I have argued that Clarence Jordan's biblical interpretation reflects his exposure to significant theological and interpretive movements of his day, along with a somewhat modernist mindset to what some would have called biblical mythology. I would like to conclude with some reflections on Jordan as a white interpreter of the Bible.

The academic conversation we now know as "whiteness studies" did not exist in Jordan's day.[33] But Jordan also lived in an era, and among communities, in which people said aloud things they would refrain from saying today. Jordan would have resisted our turning him into an object of devotion. He even cautioned against turning *Jesus* into an object of devotion. For example, evidence from Jordan's seminary days reflects a healthy dose of paternalism along with his awareness that white Christians had much to learn from the black church.[34] Moreover, Jordan's progressive racial sentiments did not convert his imagination with respect to gender.[35] Nevertheless, I strongly suspect that he and others in his day possessed insights concerning white identity that are lost to me and my generation. Jordan lived the race question, and he lived it in relationships of community and accountability with black people. Unlike many whites, Jordan directly reported the lessons he had learned from black people, and he did so without patronization.[36]

Clarence Jordan understood that race and the gospel intersected at one crucial point: at the question of loyalty. As a Bible scholar he was—as I once was—trained to practice exegesis and to flee eisegesis. In Jordan's day biblical interpreters were to set their commitments aside and pursue objectivity. It would take professional biblical scholars until the end of the twentieth century to assess and celebrate the role that factors such as culture, power, and identity play in interpretation. But Jordan understood that attention to real, flesh and blood people and their struggles constitutes

---

32. Ibid., 124–26.

33. To dabble your toes in that conversation, see Thandeka, *Learning to Be White* (New York: Continuum, 2007).

34. Marsh, *Beloved Community*, 64–65.

35. Jordan, *Substance of Faith*, 115–17. Looking back at my high school study Bible, I see that I highlighted wives submitting to their husbands and children to their parents but not slaves to their masters.

36. As in ibid., 33–34.

an essential component for interpretation.[37] The question of loyalty—and that's what the word we translate as "faith" means—determined Jordan's work as an interpreter.

Jordan's culture talked about following Jesus, but it demanded absolute fidelity to the race code. Over and again, Jordan's interpretive practices identified him as a race traitor. (They had a different term in his day.) Paul, Jordan says, was imprisoned for his position on race.[38] The Pharisees were segregationists.[39] Jews and Gentiles corresponded to whites and blacks.

As an interpreter, the single most provocative way in which Jordan committed racial treason involved the matter of Jesus' death. Jordan observed that no modern practice corresponds to Roman crucifixion.[40] His "translation" of crucifixion as lynching involves a lot more than finding a contemporary example of unjust execution. It builds a link between African Americans and their suffering with that of Jesus. Jordan's own words say as much: "They crucified him in Judea and they strung him up in Georgia, with a noose tied to a pine tree."[41]

Southern Baptist piety revolved around Jesus' death as a willing self-sacrifice, an exchange in which Jesus offered up his own life as satisfaction for the sins of humankind. When Clarence Jordan translated "crucifixion" into "lynching," he eviscerated this doctrine of penal substitutionary atonement. In its place Jesus becomes not a sacrifice but a martyr. Moreover, Jordan's translation also identified black people with Jesus and nice, religious white folk as the violent mob. Clarence Jordan knew what he was doing.

---

37. Fernando F. Segovia, "Toward a Hermeneutics of the Diaspora: A Hermeneutics of Otherness and Engagement," in *Reading from This Place*, vol. 1: *Social Location and Biblical Interpretation in the United States*, ed. Fernando F. Segovia and Mary Ann Tolbert (Minneapolis: Fortress, 1995); Francisco F. Lozada and Greg Carey, eds., *Soundings in Cultural Criticism: Perspectives and Methods in Culture, Power, and Identity in the New Testament* (Minneapolis: Fortress, 2013).

38. Jordan, *Substance of Faith*, 110.

39. Ibid., 105.

40. Jordan, *Cotton Patch Version of Paul's Epistles*, 8–9.

41. Jordan, *Substance of Faith*, 9.

4

Strangers in a Strange Land

Alternative Christian Voices in the South

———◆———

Timothy Downs

I deeply appreciate the invitation to be with you to recognize Clarence Jordan on the occasion of celebrating his one hundredth birthday. We honor a prophetic witness made well before its time, a witness which has sent ripples through history. However, I acknowledge that I am an improbable voice among you today. I am the Conference Minister of the Southeast Conference of the United Church of Christ. As a conference minister, I am a judicatory executive, you could say, a pontiff. Today I am a pontiff among prophets. As conference minister, I am called to serve an institution, to build and maintain it, imperfect though it is. A prophet is to proclaim and witness to a God given truth, to disrupt the institution, to call it back to faithfulness. As a conference minister, a pontiff, I am a keeper of order, insofar as order in the church is possible!

Prophets are men and women marching to the beat of a different drum, a discordant beat, a disrupting beat, often a disturbing and unwelcomed beat. I think of Andrew Young, who, when he arrived in Atlanta to work with the Southern Christian Leadership Conference, sought to join

First Congregational Church, United Church of Christ. He was told by the pastor, "Andy, you are welcome here, but keep that civil rights nonsense out of this church." We remember that Martin Luther King, Jr., who is now honored by a national holiday, was often not so honored during his ministry, and certainly not by his home denomination. We consider today Clarence Jordan, a man nurtured and raised in the Baptist tradition in the South, yet need we say much about how his voice for racial reconciliation was first received by the Southern Baptists of Sumter County, Georgia, in 1942?

When I settled on the title of this address as "Strangers in a Strange Land," I was thinking not only of Clarence Jordan, but also the United Church of Christ, and our particular vocation in these Southern United States. We are a denomination that was born out of the naiveté of twentieth-century ecumenism. We are the only united and uniting church in the United States, and we boldly include Jesus' words in his prayer in the seventeenth chapter of the Gospel of John, "that they may all be one" in our denominational logo. We are the merger of four distinctive denominations; the Congregationalists, Christians, the Reformed Church, and finally the Evangelical. The Congregationalists trace their roots to the Pilgrims and Puritans of New England. The Christians are the product of an early nineteenth-century American frontier revival movement. The adherents of the German Reformed Church migrated to this country from the Palatinate region of Germany from the mid-eighteenth century through the mid-nineteenth century. Finally, the members of the Evangelical Synod of North America migrated here from Prussia, and were the result of a merger between Reformed and Lutheran traditions in their homeland. What brought this union together? A strong impulse to mission and to social justice, and a conviction that in our unity we can serve those impulses more faithfully. Yet, these two vocations of seeking social justice and Christian unity are often in tension. One is a vocation of prophetic challenge, and the other a vocation of reconciliation.

Our story as a denomination in the South is largely that of our Congregational forebears. While some arrived on the South Carolina coast as early as the mid-seventeenth century, our identity was shaped largely by the work of missionaries who came into the South on the heels of Union soldiers as they swept across the South in the Civil War. Most of them were women, and they were heirs of New England abolitionists. They established over 500 schools and 200 churches to serve the newly emancipated African American citizens of the South in the last half of the nineteenth century.

They were ostracized, threatened, lynched, and hundreds died of disease. They came to make the same sacrifice for "love and light" that their brothers had made on the battlefield to preserve the Union.

When this Congregational tradition merged with the three other traditions into the United Church of Christ in 1957 they formed an improbable and some would say unsustainable witness to Christian unity. Here then is the tension. In the United Church of Christ we will affirm on one hand "one Lord, one faith, one God and (parent) of us all," which is, as I noted, a ministry of reconciliation and gathering. On the other hand we affirm the Jesus who said, "as you do this to the least of my brothers (and sisters), you do it to me," a ministry calling us to the scandal of reaching out to the marginalized and dispossessed. Some would say that the Southeast Conference of the United Church of Christ is evidence in itself of the unsustainability of this tension. When it was organized in 1966 it was comprised of 138 congregations in a five-state area, and today there are 50. From the mid-1960s to the present American culture has been buffeted by one set of social issues and then another, ranging from the struggle for racial justice to the rights of women in society, from the advocacy for peace in the 1960s, to the current struggle for the full inclusion of LGBTQ people in the life and leadership of the church. Each of these sets of issues seemed to cause another exodus of congregations from the United Church of Christ in the South. The last group of churches to leave the Southeast Conference were twelve churches in 2005. They were protesting the position taken by the General Synod of the United Church of Christ, our bi-annual national gathering of the church, in support of marriage equality for same gender-loving people. This describes in part but not in whole the reasons behind our decline. It is estimated that 80 percent of United Church of Christ churches could be described as dying.

Yet, I have hope; hope for the United Church of Christ, hope for our future, and hope for our ministries. As I look at the lives of Clarence Jordan, those who have been touched by Koinonia Farm, or Will Campbell of Nashville, Martin Luther King, Jr., Fanny Lou Hamer, John Lewis, Coretta Scott King, Dorothy Cotton, and so many others, those voices and their witness have redirected the course of history. They have done so often against great odds, but each has done so in a spirit of pervading love and an urgent quest for justice.

I had the privilege of hearing John Lewis preach recently. He spoke about a time almost fifty years ago when he, with a group of white and black students, undertook to desegregate a bus station waiting room in North Carolina. The local sheriff arrived with a band of men he had just deputized for this occasion, and they beat the occupiers relentlessly. Thirty years later Representative Lewis was in his office in the United States capital building. His secretary announced that there was a visitor to see him. The visitor entered and asked him, "Do you remember me?" John Lewis said, "No." The visitor continued, "I was the sheriff who beat you thirty years ago, and I have come to apologize." John Lewis added, "I never hated him, I do not have time to hate. He has come to visit me several times since, and we have become friends. You see," he finished, "that is the power of love."

I remember reading of Will Campbell in the height of the civil rights movement describing a visit to a northern college campus. He was showing a movie in which a formation of Ku Klux Klan members were marching and the leader commanded the group to "right march!" One of the men turned left and marched into the nearby woods. The movie's watchers broke into laughter of derision. Will Campbell flicked the lights on and said to them, "Why are you laughing? This man, so ignorant that he does not know his right from his left, is as oppressed as any by his own ignorance!"

In its imperfect way, the United Church of Christ seeks to live out this spirit of witnessing to justice, while calling me and our pastors to be more than pontiffs and priests, but prophets as well. We are to integrate in our institutional ministries the recognition that "justice is what happens when love grows legs and walks the earth," as Serene Jones, President of Union Theological Seminary, has written. In my tradition our vocations as pontiff, priest, and prophet are woven together; we are to embrace both justice and call to unity. We are to seek order and inspire disorder. Our embrace of unity is the foundation of the inclusivity which we celebrate when we recite together "no matter who you are or where you are on life's journey, you are welcome here." This is both a reconciling and prophetic act.

I said I have great hope. Why? Because the voices of Clarence Jordan and the many others who have courageously spoken are voices that have shaped a growing shift that is taking shape four and five decades later. The theologian Diana Butler Bass writes and speaks about this, referencing the work of William McLoughlin in his book *Revivals, Awakenings and Reforms*. She speaks of the five stages of cultural revitalization, and notes that in American history there have been three great awakenings, and we are now in the midst of a fourth awakening, "a massive, sustained movement of reorientation."

The First Great Awakening in American history, which dates to the middle of the eighteenth century, is best known to us through the preaching of Jonathan Edwards. He stirred a moribund church with his calls to renewal, calls with which many of us first became acquainted through his sermon, "Sinners in the Hands of an Angry God." The Second Great Awakening took place in the first part of the nineteenth century, with the rise of the abolitionism, the movement for women's rights, and prohibition, all of which had the fervor of the First Great Awakening, but now manifested an awareness that God's redemptive activity is greater than the redemption of individual souls but also present in acts of justice for the marginalized and disenfranchised. The Third Great Awakening took place at the turn of the twentieth century, and saw the rise of Christian unity, a growing appreciation of pluralism, the growing voice of the labor movement, and pacifism.

The Fourth Great Awakening, heralded by Clarence Jordan and so many others whose names are both well known and unknown, is unfolding around us. It is characterized by a valuing of religious pluralism and an appreciation of the faiths of others. There is a growing awareness that we live not in nation states as much as a global community. The environmental movement is evidence of a growing care for the earth. We are showing greater caring for one another, and seeking to build more humane economic systems not constrained by the old capitalist or socialist models, both of which have been abusive and cruel in much of their application.

Diana Butler Bass goes on to note the breakdown of traditional values. For those of us living in the Fourth Great Awakening we saw this in the rise of the civil rights movement and feminism, in the peace movement, and the environmental movement. While these shifts in societal values were taking place, we also saw "cultural distortions" in reaction to them. We heard disparaging comments about hippies, talk about the traditional family values, mutterings about the erosion of values. All this while disregarding the ways in which values of the past violated women, same gender-loving people, and people of color.

A new vision begins to take more distinctive shape, new moral and ethical possibilities begin to emerge, and prophets of this new way begin to get a wider hearing. In the more mainstream society, people begin to "get it"; conflicts become sharper and divisions between the old and new grow more pronounced. A transforming begins to unfold, and the "undecided" note the necessity of the new vision and the need for the new patterns;

institutions begin to shift, and we see political reform and new economic patterns.

There is throughout a pull forward and a push back, but throughout, a grand drama is unfolding, and in the midst of this ambiguity I remain deeply grateful for the pioneers and prophets, often lonely voices yet persistent and pressing. I belong to a people represented by the United Church of Christ, and its predecessor denominations that have been at the leading edge of each Great Awakenings, from the first to the present. My spiritual forbears have been pioneers and prophets, with names such as Jonathan Edwards, Harriet Beecher Stowe, Harry Emerson Fosdick, Reinhold Niebuhr, William Sloane Coffin; all of these in each of the Awakenings of which they were a part pried open the door a little further. Clarence Jordan and the Koinonia Partners too were among the first sparks of the Fourth Great Awakening into which we are all now living.

As a conference minister in the United Church of Christ, I seek to honor and embrace the vocation of prophet. I welcome the prophetic future that Diana Butler Bass anticipates; a world in which we have a growing appreciation for our interconnectivity; a rising global consciousness. I celebrate a growing appreciation for our religious pluralism, and an embrace of something more than tolerance, but of welcome, as we are meeting sisters and brothers of other faiths. I appreciate the ways in which we are seeking to live with greater care on our earth and our growing recognition of our dependence on this earth for our own well-being. I am grateful for those who seek to move us beyond the old and rigid models of economic systems to more flexible, humane systems that seek to embody greater justice and equity for all. Yes, we may be strangers in a strange land, yet I am grateful for the strangers who have ventured before us, with a vision in their hearts of a New Jerusalem. They inspired us today to "order our steps" on this path to greater wholeness greater justice, and greater freedom.

5

Clarence Jordan as Baptist

Celebrating the Radical Baptist Heritage

G. W. Carlson

Introduction: Clarence Jordan's Invitation to Explore a Radical Baptist Heritage

In January 1963 I had my first opportunity to interact with Clarence Jordan. I was a junior at Bethel College in St. Paul, Minnesota. His stories about a Jesus who ministered in Georgia were interesting to me. He represented a third option in the civil rights movement. Beyond securing rights within the legal system and using nonviolent protests as a tool for demanding change, Clarence Jordan advocated that the Christian church model a community that would look like the kingdom of God. Here was a person who reflected my Baptist heritage and would mobilize its core beliefs to create a demand for a "radical" expression of faith.[1]

This was the era of the early efforts to integrate Christian colleges, an effort that was not always successful. The Bethel president was at least willing to allow for diverse voices to be present on campus, including the

---

1. "Jordan to Consider Racial Tension Reply," *The Clarion*, January 15, 1963, 1.

address by Benjamin Mays at the 1957 Commencement. In 1960 Martin Luther King, Jr. was invited to speak on campus. He was eventually not able to attend because of a civil rights crisis in Atlanta.[2] Dr. Anton Pearson, a contemporary of Clarence Jordan at Southern Baptist Theological Seminary in Louisville and Professor of Old Testament at Bethel Seminary, argued for a Christian commitment to civil rights in St. Paul and endorsed a pacifist stand on war and peace issues.[3]

During my forty-four years at Bethel University I have developed and frequently taught a class entitled *Christian Nonviolence*, which attempts to explore the theological, historical, and practical implications of peacemaking as a biblical norm. Clarence Jordan helped to raise many of the core themes for this course, and I have regularly included his sermons on the Good Samaritan, radical discipleship, and Christian peacemaking in the class.[4]

The life and witness of Clarence Jordan, along with F. O. Nilsson, Isaac Backus, Francis Bellamy, Helen Montgomery, Nannie Burroughs, Walter Rauschenbusch, and Martin Luther King, Jr., has helped me to develop a paradigm for radical Baptist discipleship that encourages courageous Christian dissent. The paradigm includes the following: 1) an early identification with people in need or people who are unacceptable to mainstream societal norms; 2) a serious discontent with the witness of the established Christian church and a desire to recover a more authentic faith; 3) a desire to follow in the footsteps of Christ and faithfully to live out the principles of the Sermon on the Mount; 4) a need to develop an alternative faith community to provide a "counter-culture" Christian witness, encourage responsible discipleship, and develop collegial support networks; 5) a faith journey that integrates Christian spirituality and social and economic justice; 6) a theological commitment to the "sacredness of life" and the dangers of hedonism and materialism; and 7) a belief in a "servanthood" model of leadership.

During the past two decades "progressive Baptists" have found Clarence Jordan a valuable prophet whose critique of the issues of his day are still relevant to an understanding of the gospel in today's Christian

2. Diana Magnuson and Kent Gerber, "Martin Luther King Invited to Address Bethel Convocation," *Baptist Pietist Clarion*, vol. 10, no. 1, June 2011, 7–12.

3. Anton Pearson, "Christian Responses to Civil Rights Issues in St Paul," Bethel Seminary cassette tape, 1963.

4. G. William Carlson, "Baptist Pietist Should Celebrate the Civil Rights Movement" *Baptist Pietist Clarion*, vol. 1, no. 1, March 2002, 9–12.

communities. Although he is relevant to leaders of many traditions, he is significantly relevant for those who believe that the "Baptist" tradition must recover a radical heritage and apply it to today's challenges.

Clarence Jordan as "ex-Baptist": Calling His Baptist Fellowship to Recover a Commitment to a "Radical Discipleship"

Clarence Jordan actively engaged his Southern Baptist heritage and supported many components of its ministry. He often feared that all Christian traditions no longer reflected the incarnation of the "life, death, and resurrection of Jesus." The Southern Baptist churches with which he associated were captured by culture and had become "enclaves of racism and were concerned with petty programs of self-enhancement."

Jordan's response was well expressed in the crisis experiences that the Koinonia Farm members had with the Rehoboth Baptist Church. In August 1950 a student from India visited the Farm. He was a student at Florida State University and was intrigued with the Farm's commitment to nonviolence. He went to the Rehoboth Baptist Church with the other members of the Koinonia community. The church community "ignored" the visitor and eventually excommunicated the Jordan family and other residents of Koinonia. They were charged with "bringing a member of another race to church, regularly attending black church services, making 'remarks that seem unchristian' about the church's beliefs and publically disagreeing with 'some doctrine and practices of the church.'"[5]

Clarence told the pastor as he was being escorted out that "if we're sinners, we need to hear the word; if we're saints, we need the fellowship—in any case, we ought to be there." Clarence Jordan's statement is a clear expression of his traditional Baptist beliefs and the reality that the Rehoboth Church was the one that was denying the legitimacy of a heritage:

> It is our desire . . . that it be clearly understood that our absence would be due, not to any malice or lack of forgiveness or willingness to attend on our part, but to the will and action of the church itself. We wish to extend to the pastor, the deacons, and the entire membership our sincere sympathy in these hours of suffering. We are grieved that it has become impossible for us to walk together as brethren in the Lord Jesus. Truly both you and we have broken

---

5. Ann Louise Coble, *Cotton Patch for the Kingdom* (Scottdale, PA: Herald, 2002), 90.

His heart, and we all should penitently seek His forgiveness. It is our fervent prayer that all of us shall heed the command of our Lord Jesus to forgive each other "until seventy times seven"; to pray for one another; and to love those "who despitefully use you." May there be a ready willingness for a reconciliation which would involve no sacrifice of conscience or compromise of our Lord's truth.[6]

The Jordans would never join another church. When Jordan was asked about his denominational affiliation, he, with a twinkle in his eye, would reply, "Ex-Baptist."[7]

What does this phrase likely mean? What were the core beliefs of the Baptist heritage that Jordan had to "forsake" and did he ever really leave it? Henlee Barnette, who was professor of Christian Ethics at Southern Baptist Theological Seminary from 1951–1977 and a close friend of Clarence Jordan, attempted to define Jordan's core beliefs. Barnette valued Jordan's work at Koinonia Farm, participated in the civil rights movement, and invited him to address the Seminary for the Gheens lectures. Barnette wrote the following about Clarence Jordan's Baptist heritage:

> Originally, Clarence was nurtured in the traditional theology of Southern Baptists. But as he encountered the moral issues of racial prejudice, the plight of the poor, the draft of World War II, he felt the need for a theological framework more adequate for social passions and ethical concerns. This he had not found in either his church life or the seminary in Louisville. Both of these institutions were largely otherworldly oriented and promoted a privatized faith . . . While he may not have gained much knowledge about ethical and social issues from his teachers, he learned a lot about Koine Greek. Once, he told me with a twinkle in his eye, that he learned a lot of New Testament Greek in spite of his teachers. He discovered in the Greek New Testament a scriptural basis for his moral passion and social action.[8]

For Jordan the efforts to develop the Koinonia Community would have to challenge the five realities co-opting the Southern Baptist churches he knew and loved: the demands of a Constantinian view of political and social institutions, a domesticated understanding of the conversion experience, a

6. Ibid., 91–92.

7. Henlee Barnette, *Clarence Jordan: Turning Dreams Into Deeds* (Macon, GA: Smyth and Helwys, 1992), 22.

8. Ibid., 13–14.

recognition of a Christianity whose preeminent goal was to foster a denial of the values of the "Kingdom of God," an unwillingness to confront a church which was influenced by the "closed society of Jim Crow," and a reluctance to see the church as a living, prophetic witness of the gospel of Jesus Christ.

Charles Marsh attempts to understand Jordan's commitment to his Baptist heritage by arguing that Jordan's preeminent purpose in the establishment of Koinonia Farm was to develop a place of Christian fellowship whose "members sought to practice the 'Way of Jesus' in their daily life and work." Ultimately the purpose was to implement the principle of active reconciliation and explore its demanding implications for the community in which the Farm was established. Marsh wrote: "Reconciliation was first and foremost a quality of life in the body of Christ, a requirement of citizenship in the kingdom of God. And, as he saw it, life in the body of Christ from the perspective of Sumter County, Georgia, involved three interconnected passions: the practice of nonviolence as the moral disposition of the Gospel; the preservation, cultivation of the soil, 'God's holy earth'; and the proclamation and provision of hope to 'those who suffer and are oppressed.'"[9]

Marsh makes an effort to try to define the origins and support for this effort. He explores the impact of "radical Southern Baptists" and allies in the Anabaptist tradition. Marsh writes:

> The community evolved without clear design or direction. In the next few years, only a dozen or so men and women moved to the farm; most were like-minded Christians from Southern Baptist or Anabaptist traditions. Other people came for short visits—college students, volunteers from the Mennonite Central Committee, and a handful of Baptist radicals like Will Campbell and Foy Valentine . . .[10]

Out of these interactions came the 1951 document, which helped to define the nature of the community, and its commitment to a biblically defined set of values: "We desire to make known our total, unconditional commitment to seek, express and expand the Kingdom of God as revealed in Jesus Christ. Being convinced that the community of believers who make a like commitment is the continuing body of Christ in earth, I joyfully enter into a love union with the Koinonia and gladly submit myself to it, looking to it to guide me in the knowledge of God's will and to strengthen me in the

---

9. Marsh, *The Beloved Community* (New York: Basic Books, 2005), 69.
10. Ibid.

pursuit of it."[11] Jordan concluded that "I think our duty is to make Koinonia as nearly the body of Christ as we are able. That is our task."[12]

The thesis of this chapter is that Jordan made a good faith effort to sustain his Southern Baptist heritage and adapt it to the changing crises he encountered. His ability to do this was enhanced by a willingness to include several streams of thought and practice from the Anabaptist tradition. At no time did Jordan want to give up on his Baptist colleagues, even those from the South. He strongly believed that the Koinonia Farm Experiment, the writing of the *Cotton Patch Gospels*, and willingness to engage the civil rights movement were essentially targeted at bringing his Baptist colleagues back to a faith premised on the life and teachings of Jesus and the life of the early church.

Clarence Jordan as a Baptist: What Were His Core Identities?

Early Baptist history was framed by the development of several dissenting church communities that wished to challenge the Church of England. They emerged from the Puritan-Separatist heritage. Although there is a significant debate about the influence of the Anabaptist communities on Baptist faith commitments, there is a consensus of beliefs that emerge: the idea of believers baptism by immersion, the church as a community of believers who voluntarily associate because of their belief in a conversion experience based on the saving grace of Jesus' death and resurrection, a congregational style of worship centered around the preaching of the Word, and a commitment to evangelism and missions.

Virgil Olson, church historian for the Baptist General Conference (now Converge Worldwide) made a strong effort to define the essence of the Baptist Pietist tradition, a tradition that is compatible with Clarence Jordan's theological principles as a Baptist. Olson asserted the following core themes: 1) As a Baptist I believe that the New Testament is the final source for theology, polity, and mission, superseding all other Affirmations, Declarations, Creeds. 2) As a Baptist I believe in soul competency and liberty of conscience of a person to discern and decide for the truth as revealed in the Scriptures. 3) As a Baptist I believe in the priesthood of all believers. 4) As a Baptist I believe that membership of the church should be

11. Ibid., 70.
12. Ibid., 71.

made up of consenting, regenerate believers in Christ who have confessed their faith through baptism by immersion. 5) As a Baptist I believe that the local church is autonomous. 6) As a Baptist I believe that the membership of the local church has the final authority in making decisions. 7) As a Baptist I believe in religious liberty.

Olson adds, "Baptists believe that each individual should be free to worship God, or not worship God, according to the dictates of their own conscience. This means that we not only guard our own religious liberty, but we also are willing to support others with whom we may disagree, that they, too, may have the right to worship or not worship the way they choose."[13]

The second tradition that Clarence Jordan adopted was that of the Anabaptist heritage. Some have called the Anabaptist movement either the "left wing of the Reformation" or the "radical Reformation." The movement developed in the sixteenth century, challenging an understanding of the nature of the church in Zwingli's Zurich. The core issue was infant baptism and the methods by which one interpreted the Bible. The church needed to be free from state control. The Bible, according to leaders such as Conrad Grebel and George Blaurock, was the only basis of faith and encouraged a renewed focus on the life and teachings of Jesus, especially the Sermon on the Mount.

There were several Anabaptist traditions, from the Mennonite communities in the Netherlands to more radical expressions under the leadership of Jacob Hutter. The core beliefs were found in the Schleitheim Confession and the various state churches persecuted many of the early adherents.

What united these communities were the following core ideas: The Bible, and especially the New Testament, was the only criteria by which all faith commitments were developed; the development of the believer's church, a strong belief in religious liberty, an understanding of the necessity of "radical discipleship" as the core lived obligation of the faith communities, rejection of the church territorial, the necessity of evangelism and a vision of the church as a counter-cultural community. Anabaptist communities refused to participate in warfare, established a "communal"

---

13. Virgil Olson, "Why I'm a Baptist," *Baptist Pietist Clarion*, vol. 2, no. 1, July 2003, 4. Other works that can be consulted are David Bebbington, *Baptists Through the Centuries* (Waco, TX: Baylor University Press, 2012); Pamela Durso and Keith Durso, *The Story of Baptists in the United States* (Brentwood, TN: Baptist History and Heritage Society, 2006); and Bill Leonard, *Baptists in America* (New York: Columbia University Press, 2005).

understanding of economic relationships and encouraged a belief in the "reconciled" community, which values the sacredness of life.[14]

For Clarence Jordan, as a Baptist, evangelism was the declaration that God was engaged in changing people and changing the world. It was earlier expressed in his work with the black churches in the Haymarket area of Louisville. In these early experiments the larger church community could build interracial church communities and encourage the economic sharing of goods. The experiment of Americus, Georgia was to be a more radicalized effort. Jordan argued that the early church effectively modeled the gospel of Jesus Christ. The Koinonia experiment was designed to implement the "radical sharing of goods" as found in the early church at Jerusalem.

Clarence Jordan Articulated a Radical Baptist Heritage

Seven major principles guided Jordan's "Baptist" and "Anabaptist" influenced effort to establish a prophetic presence at the Koinonia Farm. They would frame the base of his writings and engagements with such issues as civil rights and economic justice.

Clarence Jordan's biography included the impact of several "conversion" experiences: a personal acceptance of Christ as Savior and Lord, a recognition of "racial injustice," a struggle with the peacemaking implications of the Sermon on the Mount during his days as a member of ROTC, a call to ministry, and a recognition of the value of understanding the church as community. They would be expressed in his sermons given at Baptist churches, speeches at Baptist institutions of higher education, and interactions at Baptist denominational conferences.

1. Clarence Jordan expressed a strong commitment to the transformational view of evangelism.

Jordan often uses the caterpillar imagery and the term "metanoia" to illustrate what this transformation looks like. When one is "born from above" it involves a complete transformation of one's person. This includes how one lives as a disciple who engages in the transformation of the human community and works for the development of the "beloved community."

---

14. Arthur Paul Boers, "Anabaptist Spirituality" in ed. Glen G. Scorgie, *Dictionary of Christian Spirituality* (Grand Rapids: Zondervan, 2011), 259–61. For further study one could read William Estep, *The Anabaptist Story* (Grand Rapids: Eerdmans, 1995).

Clarence Jordan defines these evangelistic ideas in his essay on the Sermon on the Mount. He writes:

> For unbelievers, Jesus had but one word: "REPENT." When he called on people to repent, he really demanded that they change their way of thinking, abandon their false concepts, forsake their wrong methods, and enter upon a new way of life. Imagine what this meant to the Pharisees whose "good behavior" and whose "trust in the Lord" assured them of divine favor.
>
> Weren't they already saved, and just about the best people God had on earth? Yet Jesus felt that of all people, these had the greatest need of changing their ways. He also told the wealthy, aristocratic, unscrupulous Sadducees to change their way of living. He called on the super-patriotic, military minded Zealots to change their attitude. He faced all these people, as he does their spiritual descendants today, with that one terrific word: repent!
>
> No one has a right, however, to call on people to change their ways unless they have a more excellent way to offer. Forsaking the wrong way is only half of repentance; accepting the right way is the other half. The call to repentance, then, must always be accompanied by the glorious announcement, "for the kingdom of God is here!" Jesus proclaimed it as "the good news." To enter it was to be saved, to find eternal life.[15]

Tony Campolo is a radical Baptist and Red Letter Bible professor and preacher who found Jordan an effective definer of a theology of evangelism. Jordan suggests that evangelism is the good news about what God is doing in the world. Campolo added that while Jordan "emphasized that evangelism includes challenging individuals to yield to Jesus, to let Jesus into their lives, and to allow the Holy Spirit to transform them into new creations, Jordan made it clear that evangelism is much more than that. For him, evangelism also proclaims what God is doing in society right now to bring about justice, liberation and the economic well being for the oppressed. Jordan called people to participate in the revolutionary transformation of the world."[16]

---

15. Clarence Jordan, "The Sermon on the Mount" in *Clarence Jordan: Essential Writings*, ed. Joyce Hollyday (Maryknoll, NY: Orbis, 2003), 107–8.

16. Tony Campolo, "Afterword" in Jordan, *Clarence Jordan's Cotton Patch Gospel: The Complete Collection* (Macon, GA: Smyth & Helwys, 2012), 429–30.

2. Clarence Jordan articulated an essential commitment to the idea of a communitarian understanding of the church.

The Koinonia experiment was designed to replicate the "radical sharing of goods" as found in the early church at Jerusalem. Clarence Jordan expresses this idea in his translation of the second chapter of the gospel of Acts:

> Sisters and brothers, give me your attention. Surely you yourselves know about Jesus, the Valdostan, a man whom God backed up with the mighty deeds, marvelous happenings, and solid evidence which he presented right before your eyes. Within the framework of his purpose and knowledge, God let you murder him by stringing him up at the hands of a mob. But then God removed the effects of death and restored him life. It just wasn't possible for him to be contained by death...
>
> Rock said to them, "Reshape your lives and let each of you be initiated into the family of Jesus Christ so your sins can be dealt with; and you will receive the free gift of the Holy Spirit. For the guarantee is to you and your relatives, as well as of all the outsiders whom the Lord our God shall invite." Rock was going down the line on other matters, too, and kept urging them on. "Save yourselves," he was telling them, "from this goofed-up society."
>
> So those who accepted his explanation were initiated, swelling the membership to about three thousand. They were all bound together by the officers' instruction and by the sense of community, by the common meal and the prayers. A great reverence came over everybody, while many amazing and instructive things were done by the officers. They were selling their goods and belongings, and dividing them among the group on the basis of one's need. Knit together with singleness of purpose they gathered at the church every day, and as they ate the common meal from house to house they had a joyful and humble spirit, praising God and showing overflowing kindness toward everybody. And day by day, as people were being rescued, the Lord would add them to the fellowship.[17]

G. McLeod Bryan develops an understanding of Jordan's communitarian values and suggests that they may have also come from his understanding of the Anabaptist community. He writes that the thrust of Christianity for Clarence was Christ incarnate in *koinonia* (the redeemed imitating Christ

---

17. Jordan, "Bursting with Holy Spirit," in *Clarence Jordan: Essential Writings*, 68–69.

in the redeemed community). In Jordan's version, Hebrews 11:1 translates: "Now faith is the turning of dreams into deeds."

Clarence's message was "bifocal: directed to the world, as a practical plan to reorganize its social structure, and directed toward evangelical Christians to remind them of the extent of the mission of Christ. Had not his own Baptist forbears been drowned, banned, and jailed for their faith? Hubmaier was thrown into the lake at Zurich, Bunyan was incarcerated eighteen years in the Bedford prison, and Williams and Holmes were whipped and banned—all these suffered from their fellow Protestant Christians. Clarence reminded his culture-conforming evangelical brethren that the Christian who intends to live like Christ must not only contend with the world but with the compromised church itself. In his own experiences he endured John 16:2–3: "They will no longer consider you members of the congregation and the time will come when the ones that kill you will think they do God a favor."[18]

3. Clarence Jordan argued for a strong belief in the idea of a "radical discipleship."

For Jordan, Henlee Barnette argued, "faith or belief in Christ means more than intellectual assent to a Christological proposition. Rather, faith is trustful obedience to God, the translation of conviction into conduct."[19] This idea of radical discipleship often meant that the church would become, in Anabaptist language, a "counter-cultural community."

Clarence Jordan makes an effort to define the meaning of "God's invitation" to his followers to become "radical disciples."

> So then, if there is a measure of mutual strength in Christ, a certain persuasiveness of love, a kind of spiritual partnership; if there is an element of genuine compassion and concern, make me completely happy by being harmonious, by having the same love, co-thinkers, people of a single purpose. Never act competitively or for self-praise, but with humbleness esteem others as above yourselves. Don't confine yourselves to your own interests, but seek the welfare of others. In this regard, you all think as Christ Jesus did.

---

18. G. McLeod Bryan, "Theology in Overalls," *Sojourners*, vol. 8, no. 12, December 1979, 10–11.

19. Barnette, *Clarence Jordan*, 15.

Though he was in a God form, he didn't think that being on an equality with God was something to be hoarded.

So he humbled himself and took on a slave form, just like any other human being. And on purpose he turned up as a man and brought himself so low that he submitted to death—even a death on the gallows. That's why God is so proud of him and has bestowed on him the name that is above every name. In homage to the name of Jesus every knee on land, sky, or sea shall bow, and every tongue shall cry out in praise to God . . . "Jesus Christ is Lord."[20]

Greg Carey develops an approach to understanding Jordan's framework on discipleship through his understanding of the Sermon on the Mount and the reading of Scriptures. He writes: "Jordan's vision of discipleship and racial reconciliation emerged from his direct encounter with the Bible. Jordan read the Bible, especially the Gospels, voraciously. And though he possessed the best scholarly training of the day and read directly from the Greek, he kept his interpretation simple. In the true Baptist spirit, Jordan wanted no human artifice to constrain his encounter with Jesus and his teachings. Jordan believed that following Jesus required one to take a radical break from preoccupation with status and wealth, to reject violence in all its forms, and to build communities of sharing and love.[21]

Jordan attempts to help his readers understand this idea through the telling of an interaction he had with an elderly Southern churchwoman. She was as "crisp with pride as a dead honeysuckle vine making her way down the aisle, her eyes telegraphing the tone of her response to his message."

Clarence "braced, and she delivered—straight from the gut level of her culture, 'I want you to know that my grandfather fought in the Civil War, and I will never believe a word you say.'"

Clarence, who was tall and gracious and Southern as a sowbelly himself, smiled and replied, "Ma'am, your choice seems quite clear. It is whether you will follow your granddaddy or Jesus Christ."[22]

---

20. Jordan, "God's Invitation to the High Road," *Clarence Jordan: Essential Writings*, 92–93.

21. Greg Carey, "Recalling Clarence Jordan: Radical Disciple," *Huffington Post*, June 3, 2011.

22. Barnette, *Clarence Jordan*, 15–16.

4. According to Clarence Jordan the church had several assignments; the most significant one was to proclaim the presence of the kingdom of God on earth as it is in heaven.

Jordan was intrigued that Christ's followers were to be the "light of the world." In his Sermon on the Mount essay he wrote the following: "For the world has no way of seeing God except through the image of Christ which is formed in the hearts of those who love and obey him. If you wish to be a part of this great witness, you must come into the fellowship and join the forces of light in their warfare against darkness. A lone Christian is not a city set upon a hill, nor will a single candle light the world. You need your sisters and brothers, and they need you. Your gifts or your good will won't suffice. You must give yourself and take your stand with Christ's people, thereby increasing the candlepower of the light of the world..."

Many people of the first century considered Jesus a lawbreaker. He didn't observe the Sabbath in keeping with their pet theories (Mark 2:23—3:6). He seemed to disregard rules about fasting (Mark 2:18). He openly defied their time-honored traditions of ceremonial cleansing of hands and cups and plates before eating (Mark 7:1–5). To people who placed the rules of etiquette above the Ten Commandments, he was a dangerous criminal. And in their thinking the worst thing he did was to associate with low-class people and actually to eat with them (Luke 15:1). Judged by Pharisaic standards, which were commonly accepted, he had no breeding, was impolite, uncouth, impious, and irreligious.

Since Jesus did not plan to establish his kingdom communities in monasteries or lonely islands, he needed to help his believers understand their relationship to their world. Obviously he was beginning a new society, a new order.[23]

According to Henlee Barnette, Jordan believed that the church is a continuation of the incarnation of the life, death, and resurrection of Jesus. Just as "Mary was pregnant with Jesus, the Son of God, so the church in a real sense is to 'give birth' to children of God, for the church is the womb in which they are conceived."[24]

Jordan, as well as the Anabaptist community, saw the church as a healing community. By healing, Jordan argued "we do not mean just the healing

---

23. Jordan, "The Sermon on the Mount," *Clarence Jordan: Essential Writings*, 121–22.
24. Barnette, *Clarence Jordan*, 21.

of the body. It means the healing of all the hurt of mankind—economic hurt, racial hurt, international hurt, all this kind of thing as well as physical hurt. The whole hurt of mankind is brought into this business of healing and we are to make it whole." One of the ways to "heal the hurt of humankind" is to provide people with capital. Fund for Humanity is an illustration of the healing effort.[25]

5. Clarence Jordan loved to talk about a "God Movement."

Jordan consistently emphasized this idea as he translated the New Testament. It becomes, for Jordan, the essence of the Christian faith. We must follow the teachings of Jesus Christ and separate ourselves from the "religious racketeers."

> Therefore, in all your dealings with people, treat them as you want to be treated. This, in a nutshell, is the essence of all our moral and religious principles.
>
> Approach life through the gate of discipline. For the way that leads to emptiness is wide and easy, and a lot of folks are taking that approach. But the gate into the full life is hard, and the road is bumpy, and only a few take this route . . .
>
> Not everyone who glibly calls me "Lord, Lord," shall enter the God Movement, but the one who does the will of my spiritual Father. The time will come when many people will gather around and say, "L-o-r-d, oh L-o-r-d, we sure did preach in your name, didn't we? And in your name we gave the devil a run for his money, didn't we? We did all kinds of stunts in your name, didn't we?" Then I'll admit right in front of everybody, "I've never known you. Get away from me, you wicked religious racketeers."
>
> That's why the one who hears these words of mine and acts on them shall be like a wise man who built his house on the rock. Down came the rain, up rose the floods, out lashed the winds. They all cut at that house, but it didn't fall. It was on rock foundation.
>
> And the one who hears these words of mine and fails to act on them shall be like an idiot who built his house on the sand. The rain came down, the floods rose up, the winds lashed out. They all cut at that house, and it fell! And my, what a collapse!

---

25. Jordan, "Koinonia in Transition," in ed. Henlee Barnette, *Clarence Jordan: Turning Dreams into Deeds* (Macon, GA: Smyth & Helwys, 1992), 52.

> When Jesus finished speaking, the people were simply amazed at his ideas, for he was teaching them like he knew what he was talking about. He didn't sound like their preachers.[26]

To be in the "God Movement" was "to incarnate in one's life the ethics of the Kingdom: the ethics of love, justice, and compassion. But these principles are abstractions until they become flesh, visible in the service of one's neighbor." To endorse the God Movement would lead to persecution because the larger world, especially the religious community, is unwilling to live as radical disciples of Christ. Therefore, even those who call themselves Christians will use their faith to legitimize actions that persecute those who are truly part of the God Movement.[27]

6. Clarence Jordan took the "peacemaking" themes from the teachings of Christ as found in the Sermon on the Mount.

Jordan discussed these ideas in his retelling of the Beatitudes, a sermon preached to a large crowd in Georgia.

> He fastened his eyes on his students and said to them:
> "The poor are God's people, because the God Movement is yours.
> "You who are now hungering are God's people, because you will be filled.
> "You who are weeping are God's people, because you will laugh.
> "You are God's people when others hate you and shun you and pick on you and blacklist you just because you bear the name of the son of man. Be happy at that time and jump for joy, your spiritual pay is high. Why, their parents did the very same to the people of God in their day.
> "BUT—
> "It will be hell for you rich people, because you've had your fling.
> "It will be hell for you whose bellies are full now, because you'll go hungry.
> "It will be hell for you who are so gay now, because you will sob and weep.

26. Jordan, "In a Nutshell," *Clarence Jordan: Essential Writings*, 43–44.
27. Barnette, *Clarence Jordan*, 22–23.

"It will be hell for you when everybody speaks highly of you, for their parents said the very same things about the phony preachers.

"But let me tell you something! Love your enemies, deal kindly with those who hate you, give your blessings to those who give you their cursing, pray for those insulting you . . . Love your enemies, and be kind, and lend, expecting nothing. And you'll get plenty of 'pay'; you'll be the spitting image of the Almighty, who is friendly towards the unlovely and the mean."[28]

Jonathan Wilson-Hartgrove attempts to define the essence of Jordan's commitment to the peacemaking tradition when he discusses how Jordan responded to the violence against the Koinonia community. Hartgrove wrote:

> I love to tell the story of how, when Jordan and his family went to South Georgia in 1942 to start an inter-racial community, the KKK showed up to visit. They asked for Jordan and told him as polite Southern gentlemen that they weren't going to let the sun set on someone like him in their town. As only he could, Jordan said, "I gave 'em my broadest smile and said, 'Pleased to meet you, gentlemen. I've been waiting all my life to meet someone who could make the sun stand still.'"
>
> When one reads the diary of Dorothy Day it is clear that this deeply committed Catholic pacifist was amazed at the manner in which Clarence Jordan responded to the daily violence. It was essential for the community to develop a national marketing scheme that would allow the community to "get the nuts out of Georgia." They also refused to respond to the Chamber of Commerce's effort to encourage them to leave. Jordan replied that to sell the land and leave would be like selling my momma. Koinonia is "always dying and always living again."[29]

---

28. Jordan, "Spittin' Image of the Almighty," *Clarence Jordan: Essential Writings*, 42–43.

29. Jonathan Wilson-Hartgrove, "Clarence Jordan and God's Movement Today," *Patheos*, July 2, 2012.

7. Clarence Jordan was a firm believer in the authority of the Bible and the use of the Bible in both issues of faith and practice.

Jordan emphasized that Christ's followers were to be doers of the word. His messages were based on the biblical accounts and given in an effort to be faithful to God's teachings. Jordan writes:

> Become doers of the word. Don't kid yourselves by being listeners only, because if you listen to the word and don't act on it, you are like a person looking at yourself in a mirror—you look yourself over, walk away, and then forget what you looked like. But when you take a good look at the mature idea of freedom and hang on through thick and thin, not being a wishy-washy hearer but a person of action, you will be really happy in your work.
>
> If you think you have religion, but can't keep from running off at the mouth, and if you have a dishonest heart, your religion is as dead as a doornail. The religion which God considers pure and clean is to look after helpless orphans and widows and to keep one's self free from the taint of materialism.[30]

Jordan always took the Baptist, Bible-centered tradition seriously. He was forever reading from his worn copy of the Greek New Testament. From this he "uncovered for his hearers the radical ethic." For Clarence the Scriptures emphasized the need to take the "free church" seriously. Within the church all were equal: young and old, black and white, male and female, rich and poor, learned and unlearned. The division between clergy and laity, between work and worship, he reminded them, did not appear in their tradition or in the Scriptures, which they honored as the sole guide of faith and practice.

Clarence Jordan writes the following about his Cotton Patch translations:

> Another reason for a "cotton patch" version is that the Scriptures should be taken out of the classroom and stained-glass sanctuary and put out under God's skies where people are toiling and crying and wondering; where the mighty events of the good news first happened and where they alone feel at home . . . With my companions along the dusty rows of cotton, corn and peanuts, the Word of Life has often come alive with encouragement, rebuke, correction and insight. I have witnessed the reenactment of one

---

30. Jordan, "Belief Backed By Deeds," *Clarence Jordan: Essential Writings*, 99–100.

New Testament event after another until I can scarcely distinguish the original from its modern counterpart."[31]

7. Clarence Jordan as "conscientious" Christian dissenter: the radical Baptist message in today's Baptist sermons

During the past several decades scholars and religious leaders have looked for "Baptist heroes" whose lives and witness can play a positive role in helping to define a radical Baptist vision for today's church. The issues remain the same: a co-opted church, a failure to advance the reality of King's "beloved community," increased inequalities in the world, which are also found in the life and priorities of today's church, consistent endorsement of an aggressive, often militaristic foreign policy, and desire to create a "privatistic" understanding of evangelism.

Jerrod J. Hugenot, pastor of the First Baptist Church of Bennington, Vermont, isolates the contemporary witness of Clarence Jordan in a sermon entitled "The Might of the Mite," which celebrates the gift of the poor widow. The story emerges after Christ's criticism of the life of the wealthy synagogues and their leaders. These leaders challenge the legitimacy of the radical gospel of Jesus Christ. They cover up their wealth and irresponsible elite status by looking pious and claiming the rewards of religious leadership.

The pastor illustrates the issues of the widow's mite in today's world by exploring the stories of twentieth century Baptist conscientious Christian leaders. He writes:

> From time to time, I recall in my sermons the witness of Baptists who identified strongly with this facet of the gospel. I note that the great "social witnesses" of Baptists (folks like Walter Rauschenbusch, Clarence Jordan, Martin Luther King, Jr.) heard the clear call of Jesus to wed "gospel" with "justice," only to experience many a cold shoulder from other Baptists who considered work among the poor and advocacy for social concerns to be less important, if at all, to the "real" work of the church. Jesus cared passionately about those who were forgotten, and yet the Church tends to keep the fuller gospel at arm's length. The widow's mite challenges us to speak with humility about our stewardship and our religious

31. Bryan, "Clarence Jordan: 1912–1969," *Voices in the Wilderness*, 60.

ideals. How do we live out the ways of Jesus, given as they are to humility, service, and care for the least of these?[32]

What is most interesting is the presence of Jordan's life and witness in the development of contemporary Baptist sermon themes. This author was able to survey more than 400 sermons from the Internet that used the life and teachings of Clarence Jordan as illustrations for their themes. From the more than 200 Baptist sermons one can develop five core themes that define a "radical Baptist" witness for today's church and show how the life and witness of Clarence Jordan is important as a role model and prophetic witness.

First is the need to restore an understanding of radical Baptist understanding of discipleship as the primary mission of the church.

Discipleship means that one takes the life and teachings of Jesus seriously. In a sermon entitled "Jesus is Calling For Disciples, Not Friends," Pastor Joe McKeever uses the illustration of Clarence's brother to help congregants understand that sometimes our discipleship loyalties are compromised by our economic priorities and our power commitments. The following story is frequently used in Baptist sermons in efforts to allow the congregation to reflect on their own discipleship loyalties.

> In the early fifties, so it is told, Clarence approached his brother Robert Jordan, who later became a state senator and justice of Georgia's Supreme Court. Clarence asked Robert to serve as legal representative of the Koinonia community. Robert responded:
>
> "Clarence, I can't do that. You know my political aspirations. Why, if I represented you, I might lose my job, my house, everything I've got."
>
> "*We* might lose everything too, Bob."
>
> "It's different for you."
>
> "Why is it different? I remember, it seems to me, that you and I joined the church on the same Sunday, as boys. I expect when we came forward the preacher asked me about the same question he did you. He asked me, 'Do you accept Jesus as your Lord and Savior?' And I said, 'Yes.' What did you say?"
>
> "I follow Jesus, Clarence, up to a point."
>
> "Could that point by any chance be—the cross?"
>
> "That's right. I follow him to the cross, but not on the cross. I'm not getting myself crucified."

---

32. Jerrod J. Hugenot, "The Might of the Might," First Baptist Church, Bennington, Vermont, November 8, 2009.

"Then I don't believe you're a disciple. You're an admirer of Jesus, but not a disciple of his. I think you ought to go back to the church you belong to, and tell them you're an admirer, not a disciple."

"Well now, if everyone who felt like I do did that, we wouldn't have a church, would we?"

"The question," Clarence said, "is, 'Do you have a church?'"[33]

McKeever, like many of his colleagues, asks the audience to explore what they might have done if they were Clarence's brother. Would you have the guts to stand up against friends, pastors, and family, risking your life, comfort, and security, to show love is winning? After reading the conversation that Clarence had with his brother, what does one think Clarence meant when he told his brother that he was not a disciple of Jesus, but just an admirer? What's the difference? Can the Christian church really encourage disciples rather than admirers of Jesus?[34]

H. Mark Ashworth, another Baptist, picks up this same theme in a sermon entitled "When Losing is Winning." Ashworth reflects on our need to take the cross of Christ seriously. Like Jesus, we must not succumb to the three temptations Jesus faced: materialism, power, and idolatry. He quotes the words of Clarence Jordan that "We'll worship the hind legs of Jesus, but never do a thing he says." Jesus, states Ashworth, "calls us to follow, not to admire from a safe distance, not to come and worship him then go and live like we want. Do you want to be a follower of Jesus? Then follow him. Plain and simple."[35]

Second, Baptists are to carry on the "prophetic" witness of the Bible by challenging the oppressive structures of the day.

These may have included, for Jordan, the need to struggle against apartheid, to challenge the oppressive realities of segregation, and to reject the growing inequities of the economic system. Douglas Murray, pastor of First Baptist Church, in Wilson, North Carolina, addresses these issues through an analysis of challenges of the prophet Jeremiah. He calls Clarence Jordan a modern-day prophet whose work at Koinonia challenged the "oppressive" realities of southern Georgia. Jordan argued that the primary

---

33. Joe McKeever, "Jesus is Calling for Disciples, Not Friends," First Baptist Church, Kenner, Louisiana, n.d.

34. Ibid.

35. H. Mark Ashworth, "When Losing is Winning," Union Cross Baptist Church, Kernersville, North Carolina, March 12, 2006.

witness of the church was to model an alternative community and seek out works of ministry that define the faith community as justice seekers.

Murray admires the emergence of Habitat for Humanity as an expression of the refusal of the Koinonia community to accept inequalities and respond with some practical remedies. Murray states:

> Their founder Clarence Jordan died of a heart attack one day when he was off in his personal study shack where he would write his translations of the New Testament. But the community continued and became the seedbed for a new ministry that had a dream of decent housing for people who have been living in shacks. The idea was to partner poor families that were willing to save a down payment and work on the building and pay the mortgage—to match them with other people who would contribute their own labor and other contributions. Poor people working to better themselves. Richer people willing to use their power and wealth for others instead of themselves. Habitat for Humanity spread around the world. And a little Georgia town named Americus, that once was a hotbed of racial persecution, is now the center of a worldwide ministry dedicated to the dream of no more shacks.[36]

Third, there is the call for the development of a Baptist peacemaking commitment that would challenge the militarization of American foreign policy and explore nonviolent methods of conflict resolution.

Kyle Childress, pastor of the Austin Heights Baptist Church, is one who believes that Clarence Jordan is a "hero of faith."[37] In a sermon entitled "Seeing the Lord," he expounds on the role of forgiveness as part of a peacemaking lifestyle. By forgiving and living peaceably we give witness to the practice of reconciliation and give evidence of the resurrection of Jesus Christ. Childress tells the following story concerning Clarence Jordan's response to a fellow church member who wanted reconciliation. This church member had been part of the effort to excommunicate the Jordans from the local Baptist church because of their racial and economic positions. Childress states:

> Florence Jordan, the widow of Clarence Jordan, over thirty years ago told me of the time about two weeks after she and Clarence had been kicked out of the nearby Baptist church because of their

---

36. Douglas Murray, "A Burning Fire in My Bones," First Baptist Church, Wilson, North Carolina, August 15, 2004.

37. Kyle Childress, "Seeing the Lord," Austin Heights Baptist Church, Nacogdoches, Texas, April 15, 2012.

work across racial lines. Clarence and Florence started and lived on Koinonia Farm down in South Georgia. Florence remembered that she was in the kitchen when there was a knock on the screen door and a man from that church was there asking for Clarence.

About that time Clarence came up from working on a tractor and asked how he could help the fellow. The man said, "Clarence I can't sleep at night and I came to see if you could help. You see, I can't sleep because I keep hearing singing all night long. This singing goes on and on, and I think its angels singing, Clarence. And do you know what they are singing? They are singing, "Were you there when they crucified my Lord?" The man went on, "And Clarence, I was there. I was there two weeks ago when we voted you out of the church. Clarence, can you help me?"

Florence said that Clarence put his hand on the fellow's shoulder and said, "I forgive you." And the man began to weep. He said, "Will you ask the Lord to forgive me, too, Clarence?" And Clarence said, "No, I won't ask the Lord to forgive you, for you, but I'll tell you what I will do. I will go with you while you ask the Lord to forgive you." And Florence said that Clarence and the man went out in the yard and knelt at the foot of an old oak tree . . . and they prayed together and were reconciled. They were reconciled to God and to one another. That's a resurrection story.[38]

Fourth, there is the Baptist recognition of the church as a community, which includes people from all economic, ethnic, and educational backgrounds who are engaged in social and economic justice.

Keith Herron, pastor of the Holmeswood Baptist Church in Kansas City, Missouri, preached a sermon entitled "Leaving Everything to Follow Jesus." Jesus, states Herron, preached a theology of repentance that required the disciples to follow him and to "put down your nets because I want to teach you to fish for people" (Matt 4:19). There is a cost to be a follower of Jesus and it requires each of us to live out a "divine freedom." This freedom requires "Christ followers" to break the cycle of racism and poverty. The church must model the kingdom of God and not endorse the status quo of the powers of the world

In order to illustrate the nature of this "cost" of discipleship Herron tells one of the oft-told stories of Clarence Jordan.

> Clarence Jordan tells the story of the time in the late 1950s [when] he had been invited to preach to a North Carolina mill-town church that had been swallowed up by the city's industrial growth.

38. Ibid.

The thing that stood out for him was that the church would seat about 300 and he guessed that there must have been 600 people there and it was an even mix of folks, both blacks and whites. He also noticed that they were sitting anywhere they wanted, blacks and whites together, both in the choir and in the sanctuary.

At the end of the service, the pastor got up and said, "Now, we're going to have dinner on the grounds." The choir sang, "Let Us Break Bread Together," and then they all went outside for a dinner-on-the-grounds picnic. Jordan really trembled then because it was one thing for them to worship together, and it was quite another thing for them to eat together. He thought for sure that they would all go out back, behind the church, but they didn't. Instead they spread their food out on tables right out on the front lawn of the church, where the whole town could see them.

Jordan went over to the pastor, and said, "You know, this is a rather amazing thing to me. Were you integrated before the Supreme Court decision?" The pastor said to him in return, "What decision?" He went on to explain, "Well, back during the Depression, I was a worker here in this little mill town. I didn't have any education. I couldn't even read and write. I got somebody to read the Bible to me, and I was moved and I gave my heart to the Lord, and later, I felt the call of the Lord to preach. This little town here was too poor to have a preacher and I just volunteered. They accepted me and I started preaching. Someone read to me in there where God is no respecter of persons, and I preached that." Jordan said, "Yeah, how did you get along?"

"Well," he said, "the deacons came around to me after that sermon and said, 'Now, brother pastor, we not only don't let a nigger spend the night in this town, we don't even let him pass through. Now, we don't want that kind of preaching you're giving us.'" Again, Jordan asked, "What did you do?"

"Well," he said, "I fired them deacons." "How come they didn't fire you?" Jordan asked. "Well," he said slowly, "They never had hired me. I just volunteered."

"Did you have any more trouble with them?" Jordan continued. "Yeah. They came back at me again." "What did you do with them that time?"

"I turned them out. I told them anybody that didn't know any more about the gospel of Jesus than that not only shouldn't be an officer in the church, they shouldn't be members of it. I had to put them out."

Jordan asked, "Did you have to put anybody else out?" "Well, I preached awfully hard, and I finally preached them down to two.

> But . . .," he said, "those two were committed. I made sure that any time after that, anybody who came into my church understood that they were giving their life to Jesus Christ and they were going to have to be serious about it. What you see here is the result of that."[39]

Herron concludes that being a follower of Jesus Christ is "a calling that demanded a total commitment of body and soul to being faithful to the calling of God. In this setting it means developing a church community that breaks the power of sin and oppression."[40]

Fifth, is the strong Baptist belief in the concept of "regeneration."

Joel Snider, pastor of First Baptist Church in Rome, Georgia, preached a sermon entitled "Repent! The Kingdom of God is at Hand." Snider asks what is the meaning of a biblical concept of repentance and how is it found in Jesus life and teaching? How is my life different because I believed in Jesus Christ? In what ways has the acceptance of Christ as Lord and Savior transformed my values and commitments?

Snider uses the ideas of Clarence Jordan on this theme of "repentance" to help his congregation to understand the radical nature of being a member of the kingdom of God.

He states that the "word repentance actually means to *change your mind*. In the Greek, it is *metanoia*. Meta means change and *noia* means knowledge or mind."

> Clarence Jordan, the great Georgian who translated the New Testament into the vernacular of the rural South, says it is a little like metamorphosis. Do you remember when we went to school and the teacher would have a cocoon? I don't know where the teacher got those. I have been looking for them all my life and I can hardly ever find them. The teacher would have a cocoon, and we would wait, and wait, and wait. Then, one day that butterfly would start to burst through.
>
> Clarence Jordan said, "Nobody said to that caterpillar, 'You poor little caterpillar. You are going to have to metamorphosis. You are going to have to change. You are going to quit being a worm that crawls around and you are going to be a beautiful butterfly that can fly."

---

39. Keith Herron, "Leaving Everything to Follow Jesus," Holmeswood Baptist Church, Kansas City, Missouri; EthicsDaily.com January 28, 2011.

40. Ibid.

No, everybody says, "This is the most wonderful thing I have ever seen. This is grand. This little slug that crawled along all of a sudden has been changed. It is pretty and it is beautiful. It brings us the sense of God's wonder. Metamorphosis—change form. Metanoia—change your mind and repent.

Clarence always said that the same joy for the caterpillar to become a butterfly should be the same joy that we talk about when we talk about metanoia. Changing our hearts; changing our minds; repenting; getting rid of all the filth; getting rid of all the things that would stand between us and God.[41]

One of the results of this repentance is a challenge to the values of the world that are in conflict with the values of the Kingdom of God. Lives have been changed by the saving grace of Jesus Christ. Gail Coulter, retired pastor of the Cooperative Baptist Fellowship of North Carolina church start in Hendersonville, Texas, suggested in a sermon "How Much Does a Cross Cost?" that each of us must be willing to take on the cross of Jesus. "Baptism declares your being baptized into Christ's death and resurrection. The cross leads to life—abundant life as well as eternal life. Jesus' invitation to cross-bearing is bent on giving your abundant living to God, being like Christ, losing selfishness in loving others. Jesus calls to follow him not begrudging one moment of spiritual discipline or surrender but following Jesus simply for the love of God."

Coulter illustrates this reality by telling this story that involved Clarence Jordan. "One day Clarence Jordan toured a lovely church with a fellow seminarian whose congregation had constructed the building. It was a structure of beauty, certainly calling folks into worship and even service. Jordan followed his friend through the building which would conclude with viewing the final glorious climax of the tour. Once outside the friend asked Jordan to behold the top of the church to view the magnificent gold cross. The friend said, "That cross cost $10,000." Jordan replied, "Hmm, time was when a Christian could get one of them for nothin.'"[42]

---

41. Joel Snider, "Repent! The Kingdom of God is at Hand," *EthicsDaily.com*, March 15, 2011.

42. Gail Coulter, "How Much Does a Cross Cost?" Hendersonville, Texas, n.d.

8. Clarence Jordan as Baptist: A Baptist Witness for the Twenty-First Century

Two leading Baptist professors of Christian ethics have taken on the challenge of recovering a Baptist perspective on Christian ethics. David Gushee and Glen Stassen have found Clarence Jordan a helpful role model in the development of a contemporary radical Baptist witness. David Gushee is currently the Distinguished University Professor of Christian Ethics and the Center for Theology and Public Life at Mercer College. Assisted by Glen Stassen, he developed a view of a Baptist tradition that was rooted in a serious study of Scripture, centered on Jesus Christ, historically sensitive, socially engaged, and politically active. The goal is to produce Christian disciples who will discern the signs of the times and live faithfully in and for Jesus Christ. The goal of higher education was to encourage the development of Christian radicals.[43]

In a short article on the topic "Baptists, the Economy and Violence: What is Happening and Why?" Gushee suggests that Baptists have three resources for a helpful discussion. They are: 1) We believe in a transcendent God who holds everyone accountable, and a loving Savior who comforts those in distress. 2) We have a heritage that knows something about economic ethics. 3) We have a peacemaking heritage that we must mobilize. Gushee concluded that: "We follow Jesus, who taught peace, exemplified peace, blessed peacemakers, and died to make peace between God and the world. Baptists like Clarence Jordan, Martin Luther King, Jr., Jimmy Carter and Glen Stassen have been among our nation's leading peacemakers. Our churches need to dig deep into their legacy, and our own heritage, and teach Baptists and whoever will listen that solutions to our personal, social, and national problems will not come out of the end of a gun."[44]

Glen Stassen, a native Minnesotan, whose father was a distinguished governor of Minnesota and an author of the first draft of the United Nation's charter, was schooled at University of Virginia and Southern Baptist Theological Seminary at Louisville, where he valued the input of such

---

43. David Gushee, "Developing 'Conservative Radicals' in Christian Higher Education," *Christian Higher Education*, August 14, 2008. http://www.abpnews.com/opinion/item/3475-opinion-developing-%E2%80%98conservative-radicals%E2%80%99-in-christian-higher-education#.Ut3EJhA07Z4.

44. David Gushee, "Baptist, the Economy and Violence: What is Happening and Why?" *Baptist History and Heritage*, 2009. http://www.baptisthistory.org/gusheespeaks.pdf.

teachers as Henlee Barnette and Eric Rust. While at Southern he met Clarence Jordan, who visited Barnette's ethics class. There Jordan said in 1958 that "segregation is a dying horse. A dying horse may kick convulsively now and then. It can still do some damage to those who oppose it. But its time is over. It really is dying."

Stassen valued the work of Clarence Jordan. In an essay on the Sermon on the Mount, Stassen expresses appreciation for Jordan's commitment to the value of an incarnational, trinitarian ethic and living a life of compassion. A passage in the Sermon on the Mount reads "joyful are those who practice compassion in action, for they will receive God's compassion." Stassen concludes:

> The Greek word for "compassion in action" here, *eleemones*, usually translated "merciful," means generous in doing deeds of deliverance. Mercy is about a generous action that delivers someone from need or bondage. Clarence Jordan writes: "By the merciful he means those who have an attitude of such compassion for all people that they want to share gladly all that they have with one another and with the world." Mercy in the Gospels can mean forgiveness that delivers from the bondage of guilt, or (more often) healing or giving that delivers from the bondage of need. Jesus does not split forgiveness from deeds of mercy; they are all part of God's mercy. As Jesus walks down the road and a blind or crippled person calls out, "Have mercy on me," the person does not mean "Let me off easy" or "Forgive me" but "Heal me; deliver me from my affliction." This is why in Matthew 6:2 doing mercy, *eleemosynen*, means giving alms for the poor.[45]

Larry Swain in his analysis of the distinguished work of Henlee Barnette, a strong advocate of the ideas of Clarence Jordan within the Southern Baptist tradition, suggests that there is a need for contemporary Baptist leaders to hold in reverence those who have courageously paved the way for the expression of the radical Baptist witness in today's world. There is a need not to lose the stories of those "courageous" leaders of the past who have transformed the Baptist principles into discipleship activism. The works of Walter Rauschenbusch, Howard Thurman, Martin Luther King Jr., Foy Valentine, Jimmy Allen, Henlee Barnette and Clarence Jordan need to be studied in Baptist seminaries. They are lost in seminaries that instead promote a culture of consumerism and right wing politics.

45. Glen Stassen, *Living the Sermon on the Mount* (San Francisco: Jossey-Bass, 2006), 54.

Swain declares that unless we build "a new tradition of prophetic consciousness that challenges our culture in institutions supported by the Cooperative Baptist Fellowship, we risk losing an emerging generation that knows little more than the names of these giants of social consciousness . . . Our time is short. Our resources are limited. But with resolve and commitment, we must rebuild a tradition that made a difference, not only in America but the world, as a 'light set on a hill' that the good news of Jesus Christ is a message that transforms both individuals and the social and political systems of this world with justice, mercy and peace. The best honor we can give these men and women of the past is to build on what they taught with a twenty-first-century Christian ethic that is shaped by free and faithful Baptists."[46]

It is clear that Jordan began his work as a member of the Southern Baptist community. He always intended to remain a member. His disappointment at the dangerous compromises that he experienced within the Southern Baptist Church convinced him that the best way to be a prophetic witness was to create a truly Christian community that was significantly influenced by the historic, radical Baptist heritage. A study of the life and witness of Clarence Jordan is an important story for today's Baptists. The "ex-Baptist" will always remain a "hero of faith." His life expresses well the paradigm of conscientious Christian discipleship and is an encouragement to today's radical Baptist community.

---

46. Larry Swain, "Henlee Barnette: Prophetic Practitioner," *Christian Ethics Today*, vol. 61, December 27, 2010, 6.

Nora Tisdale—The Local Theology and Folk Art
of Clarence Jordan's Preaching (Volume I)

Vincent Harding—Loving Respect, Clear Disagreement (Volume I)

Charles Marsh—At Work in the Fields of the Lord:
Clarence Jordan as Prophet of Radical Ordinariness (Volume I)

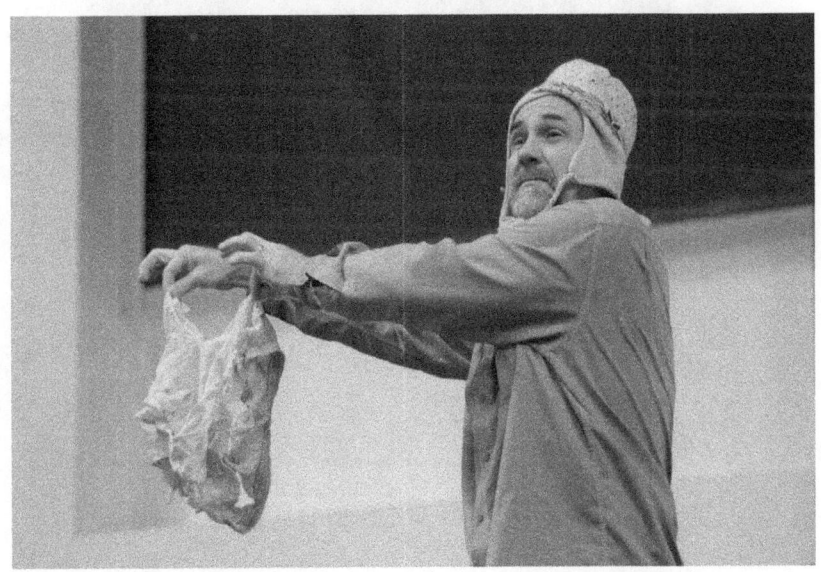

Ted Swartz – Rooted in the Cotton Patch Interview (Volume II)

President Jimmy Carter—Opening Remarks (Volumes I and II)

Sam Mahone—Reflections on the Americus Movement (Volume I)

Shane Claiborne—Tearing Down Walls (Volume II)

6

At Work in the Fields of the Lord

Clarence Jordan as Prophet of Radical Ordinariness

CHARLES MARSH

In August of 1956, in the ninth month of the Montgomery bus boycott, Martin Luther King, Jr., received a letter from a white supporter named Ernest Morgan, informing him of the recent assaults on Koinonia Farm, an intentional community near Americus, Georgia. Intentional or experimental communities had flourished in the South for at least two decades, though none had attracted as much hostility from local residents as the community near Americus. At Koinonia, Christian radicals in pursuit of racial reconciliation lived in total community, taking vows of poverty and practicing the common pursuit. Morgan was not a resident of Koinonia. He was a successful book publisher and a patron of the religious left. He had once served as the chairman of the Ohio Socialist Party and worked for a Quaker organization administering relief for Palestinian refugees in the Gaza Strip. His interests now lay in racial reform.

Morgan informed King that workers at Koinonia, with profits from their vegetable markets and roadside stands, had chipped in an hour's pay earlier in the year to help support the Montgomery Improvement

Association. But now, Morgan added, white people in Sumter County had begun applying the same strategies against the residents of the interracial farm, boycotting an institution they considered to be an offense against the southern way of life.

The nights were electric with fear: shots rained on the farm from speeding cars and Koinonians were attacked and beaten on the streets of Americus and in other nearby towns. Terrorists bombed buildings on the property, burned crosses, and vandalized and destroyed the roadside markets. Koinonia children were ostracized by their classmates at school when they weren't being bullied; some had to be sent away to live with friends and relatives in safer places. The front gate of the Farm, beneath the defaced Koinonia sign, which bore the image of a black and white hand clasped in friendship, became a depository for hostile letters, notes, and missives. One item, retrieved by a small child, announced in large letters penciled on the blank side of an Easter bulletin, "GET OUT YOU MONGRELS." And since no southern terrorist campaign would be complete without the KKK, seventy cars of klansmen arrived in caravan one night to tell the Koinonians they needed to sell the farm and move elsewhere. Meanwhile, in the light of day, business owners (including Jordan's dentist) and shopkeepers refused the patronage of Koinonians, and the farm moved front and center in a slate of official and unofficial investigations of subversive and un-American activities in the state. Atlanta Cotton States Mutual even cancelled its insurance coverage of the farm, and Jordan found himself, the son of a banker, unable to find a bank that was willing to issue loans, extend credit or retain accounts. In time, the members of the Chamber of Commerce piled in their cars for a visit of their own and offered encouragement to sell the farm and leave the area. To Citizens Councilers concerned about Koinonia's leftward leanings, Jordan tried explaining the difference between Jesus and Marx, hoping to reassure the group that he was a follower of the former not the latter; but, as Jordan would later explain, it was clear they didn't know much about either.

In May of 1958, the Governor of Georgia signed a bill authorizing a formal investigation of the farm and a series of hearings. The state representative from the south Georgia town of Dublin called Koinonia a threat to "our whole stand on segregation," and said "something ought to be done about it." The only local support for the embattled Christian community came when a ministerial association drafted a declaration against violence and called for respect of differences and protection of lives and property.

Jordan appreciated the declaration, however belated it was in coming, but at the same time accepted the growing opposition to his work as an affirmation that he was doing the right thing. A mark of the Christian was being persecuted for righteousness's sake.

Word of Koinonia's travails eventually reached religious and human rights organizations and publications outside the south—articles appeared in *The Christian Century, The Nation, The New York Times*—and petitions for prayer, expressions of solidarity and assistance in fundraising made their way into an expanded network of pastors and peace workers. Groups calling themselves "Friends of Koinonia" sprung up around the nation, organizing vigils and raising money. Some even came to Georgia to help during the season of boycott and terror. Dorothy Day, the founder of the Catholic Worker Movement, paid Koinonia a visit during her 1957 tour of the South, and stood guard one night, barely escaping with her life after being fired on in a drive-by shooting. "I will not be afraid for the terror by night nor for the arrow that flieth by day," she wrote prayerfully from Koinonia in her journal. The result was that national support of the farm and its products increased dramatically, especially the new mail-order pecan business advertised under the banner, "ship the nuts out of Georgia."

Retail merchants, seed salesmen, the fertilizer company, and auto dealers all had begun closing their doors to these strange Christians working the red-clay fields of south Georgia and dreaming of reconciled community, and the farm's insurance providers began canceling policies one by one until not even the tractors were covered. Even the crop duster crew joined the protest and refused their services.

Morgan's plea to King for help in assisting the victims of the Sumter County boycott offers a fascinating glimpse into an experiment in radical Christian community that has remained largely ignored by civil rights scholars and yet plays a prominent role in the consideration of the civil rights movement as theological drama.

The story of Koinonia Farm introduces us to the search for beloved community shaped solely by the bold venture of claiming biblical resources and descriptions of early Christian practices to create alternative social structures and practices in contemporary justice struggles. That the story also introduces us to an experiment in faith-based socialism indicates the extent to which most discussions on faith-based organizing have not fully appreciated their own radical origins.

Morgan wrote to King:

> You have probably heard of Koinonia Farm, Route 2, Americus, Georgia. Founded [fourteen] years ago by a southern white Baptist minister who was expelled from his church for preaching racial equality. [This] farm applies Christianity directly in the form of racial equality and common ownership, and, like your movement, is dedicated to non-violence. It has grown now to include 1100 acres and about 50 men, women and children. It is an efficient outfit, well equipped with houses, barns, trucks, tractors, and modern irrigation. It has, also, of course, a nice big mortgage.
>
> As its strength and influence grew and its interracial habits became better known, Koinonia has come under severe attack by southern reactionaries. To have an operation like this carried on in the deep south, by white southerners, would badly undermine their position. Not only has Koinonia run an inter-racial children's camp and accepted a Negro family in membership, but lately one of the leaders, a graduate of the University of Georgia, sponsored a Negro candidate for that institution....
>
> One of the most dangerous threats is the gradually tightening boycott against the farm products. While Koinonia has many friends and enjoys a good business reputation, its enemies are slowly but surely cutting off its markets. It is at this point that your organization might help. Your members [would] buy food. Might it not be possible for a special committee to be formed to work out some arrangement with Koinonia? Perhaps wholesale connections might be found, or possible [sic] a weekly food market could be set up. That would have to be worked out. It would mean a lot to the spirit of your members to extend fellowship and aid to a group of hard-pressed white southerners who are fighting the same battle. And it would strengthen them, both financially and morally. I might mention that my younger son has spent the summer at Koinonia without pay, driving tractors and doing other farm work, to help pull them through.

A few days later, King replied to Morgan, expressing admiration for "the noble work that is being done there." King assured Morgan that he would do everything possible to assist the farm during its crisis. Over the next two years, the "Koinonians" (as members of the community called themselves) would be received warmly by Dexter parishioners on their numerous visits to Montgomery lending support to the protest, and members of King's congregation—including Martin and Coretta—would offer hospitality and modest financial assistance for their spiritual kin in south Georgia. King would write directly to Clarence Jordan, the white Southern Baptist preacher who founded Koinonia, offering his sympathies for the "indignities and injustices that you are now confronting" and his generous hope that "you will gain consolation from the fact that in your struggle for freedom and a true Christian community you have cosmic companionship." Periodically a group of Dexter parishioners would make the two-hour drive to Koinonia to share a meal and offer encouragement of their own. It is unknown whether a special committee was formed at Dexter.

Two years later, in April of 1958, King invited Clarence Jordan to give a series of lectures on "The Church and the Kingdom of God." "We have not recently had any real discussion on the church," King wrote. King's hope was that his white preacher colleague would help the people in Montgomery "take new courage and be inspired to do [even] greater work." The converging paths of these uncommonly intense Baptist preachers for a few evenings in the spring of 1958 illuminate a broadened field of church-based racial reform in the South.

At that point, Jordan and King had never met in person. But having visited with other Koinonians in the Montgomery parsonage and in the coffee hour after church, King had come to admire the Jordans' pioneering work in Baptist racial reform. He may well have counted them among those "fearless souls" helping to create the atmosphere for the movement emerging in the South.

In fact, King's dream of beloved community, rendered immemorially in his 1963 address at the March on Washington, may have evoked the Koinonia story, the image of white and black people sitting down at a picnic table in south Georgia acting like kin. For their part, Jordan and the Koinonians had prayed regularly for the Negro church people during the year of the bus protest, grateful for their bold demonstration of Christian pacifism, and, Morgan mentioned in his letter, providing occasional financial assistance. The two pastors born and raised in Georgia shared not only a common commitment to racial reconciliation but also the conviction that the South as a region of deep faith offered unique resources for building beloved community. The pastors shared a common hope in Christian faith's power to redeem the social order. Jordan focused his lectures on the themes of the "Church and the Kingdom," the "Church as a Revolutionary World Order," and the "Church in God's Plan for the Ages."

Like King, Jordan had been influenced by the theology of the social gospel as taught by Walter Rauschenbusch (1861–1918), an American theologian who had revived the doctrine of the kingdom of God in his enterprise of mobilizing Protestants for social justice. Rauschenbusch believed that without a vital conception of kingdom of God, Christians were forever inclined to retreat into private virtuousness and otherworldly piety. But with a renewed kingdom-theology, faith would become socially engaged and compassionate; for the kingdom of God "is the energy of God realizing itself in human life." As Rauschenbusch explained in his influential book, *A Theology for the Social Gospel*, the social gospel involves "the redemption of social life from the cramping influence of religious bigotry, from the repression of self-assertion in the relation of upper and lower classes, and from forms of slavery in which human beings are treated as mere means to serve the ends of others . . .[;] the redemption of society from political autocracies and economic oligarchies; the substitution of redemptive for vindictive penology; the abolition of constraint through hunger as part of the industrial system; and the abolition of war as the supreme expression of hate and the completest cessation of freedom."

On the first night of the series, Jordan described the kingdom of God as a living, moving reality, dynamic and unsettling. Jesus never offered an easy definition of the kingdom, but instead used parables to describe it as a new way of life, a fellowship, a family, a movement. "The Kingdom of heaven is like yeast that a woman took and mixed into a large amount of flour until it worked all through the dough." Jordan took pains to distinguish the kingdom of God from the "sanctuary," or the institutional church, which bore little resemblance to the new order proclaimed in the Gospels.

Rauschenbusch had emphasized the false and tragic identification of the kingdom and the church, wherein people began to think that they were serving the kingdom by "cementing a strong church organization." But Jordan went even further, saying that the "Christ of the fields and the marketplaces" has been "entombed in cathedrals and holy places" and "rendered innocuous by making him Lord of the lips and the hymnbooks." It was the responsibility of Christian radicals like the Koinonians and the Montgomery church people to free Christ from his ecclesial shackles. Martin King must have offered a hearty "amen" to Jordan's refrain that Jesus had not come to start a religion but a revolution.

The spring lecture series was a success. The next week King wrote Jordan enthusiastically, "Words are inadequate to express my appreciation to you for the great contribution you made, not only to the Dexter Avenue Baptist Church, but to the Montgomery community, during our spring lecture series." King called the messages "profound and inspiring," the "finest series we have had in our pastorate here at Dexter." He encouraged Jordan and the other Koinonians to call on him anytime and passed along the greetings and blessings of Coretta. "You are always in my prayers," he wrote.

Sadly the exchange produced no lasting friendship. There would be no interracial speaking tours or evangelistic campaigns modeled on Billy Graham's successful crusades, at the time attracting enormous audiences in the cities of the South. The next year King left his Dexter pastorate to work full-time for the Southern Christian Leadership Conference, leaving his one and only tenure as a parish pastor, while Clarence Jordan, despite his harsh and exceedingly prescient judgments on the white evangelical church, came to a notion of Christian community so extreme in its rigor and discipline that it risked becoming as insular and obsessed with purity as the segregated churches he loathed. The differences between the two ministers then intensified. From King's perspective, Koinonia Farm simply became irrelevant to racial reform in the South, to the massive legal changes necessary for a more just nation. From Jordan's perspective, King became a parody of his former self, the man of nonviolence who relied on the men of great violence for his well being, a politician (and not a very good one) whose pastoral energies were long spent.

No doubt, as the new civil rights leader, King had little choice but to broaden his scope, fortify his leadership, and forge ahead into complex political terrain. But as a professional organizer with a staff position in his father's church in Atlanta, King was no longer accountable to the Dexter Deacons of the world, proud church people who kept his feet to the fire on moral rectitude. One of King's successors at Dexter would tell the story of how his own wrinkled shirts became a source of anguish to the Robert Nesbitt family in the first weeks of his pastorate. Rebecca Nesbitt, the Deacon's wife, became so distraught one night, that unable to sleep, she drove to the parsonage early Sunday morning, woke up the new pastor, and insisted on pressing his shirt and pants—and she had brought along her own iron and ironing board. King's new freedom to operate must have no doubt felt liberating after years of negotiating the scrupulous Dexter crowd; but in Jordan's estimation it was a freedom purchased with a moral cost. "Hectic activity," a pastor-friend had written to King, "i[s] not necessarily an indication that the cause of the Kingdom is being promoted."

Jordan believed that the only way authentic change could transpire in southern race relations was as a result of "incarnational evangelism," and that meant making Christian truth concrete in community lived and shared with the excluded and the oppressed. Evangelism at its highest,

Jordan said, is "based not upon a sermon, not upon a theory, not upon an abstraction, but upon the Word of God become flesh and dealing with us, and restoring us to our right minds." "Taking out one bunch of politicians and putting in another will not bring about the Kingdom of God," he said. "That would be kind of like exchanging a mule that's blind in his right eye for one that's blind in his left eye. A revolution based on bread would dissipate as well. If we abolish all slums and all poverty, and provide free medical care and social security for all, we still won't have the kingdom." In short, soul-regeneration—and having that born again experience transform the whole self—was key to the transformation of race relations in the South and nation.

Having been nourished as a seminarian on social gospel hopes, Jordan was not suggesting that slums and poverty not be abolished, or that federal agencies not play a role in their abolition. He rather believed himself to be retrieving a more radical faith, one exemplified in the socialism of early Christian communities; one which revealed humanity's true history, a history without violence, competitive assaults on human dignity, and the principle of "what is mine is mine." Still, for Jordan, socialism as a political achievement could never yield the kingdom of God. Socialism might serve as an allegory of the kingdom or as a reflection of the kingdom in history, but the socialist movement could not produce God's new order. Jordan was not speaking disingenuously when, under investigation by anti-communist agencies, he denied socialist or communist intentions in the experiment of Koinonia; he believed that the kingdom of God finally exploded the hard shell of politics from the inside out. Over against socialism as an ideological system, the ultimate meaning of history flowed from the "deep, rich fellowship" of God's love; and only this fellowship could enable real social change, heal the wounds of injustice, overcome oppression, and renew the earth.

Early in his ministry, Jordan preached a sermon in a small Baptist church on the white southerner's responsibility to the Negro. He had taken as his proof text a passage from Paul's Epistle to the Galatians. "For ye are all the children of God by faith in Christ Jesus. For as many of you as have been baptized into Christ have put on Christ. There is neither Jew nor Greek, there is neither bond nor free, there is neither male nor female: for ye are all one in Christ Jesus." At the conclusion of the service, an elderly woman made her way down the aisle, "as crisp with pride as a dead honeysuckle vine," Jordan later recalled. The woman was furious with Jordan for his harsh words for the South and his irreverence towards its time-honored customs. "I want you to know that my grandfather fought in the Civil War," she told him, "and I will never believe a word you say." But Jordan had seen it coming and was ready with an answer. "Well ma'am, I guess you've got to decide whether to follow your granddaddy or Jesus." Jordan was a man who understood the deep loyalty of his region to a cluttered pantheon of cultural gods.

In the plains of southwest Georgia, credentialed as a farmer and a preacher, Jordan settled in for the long haul. "Tall, high-hipped, hands jammed into blue-jean pockets, floppy stray hat shading a grin—dusty from the peanut rows, greasy from the tractor shop, bespectacled from persistent study," wrote his first biographer Dallas Lee, "Clarence Jordan was a gentle man who thundered." Jordan launched a soil conservation program by terracing the land to create greater water retention and preserve the topsoil. He experimented successfully with the technique of using ground-up peanut vines as fertilizer for the next season's crops. He established a "cow library" that enabled poor families to check out a milch without charge and to keep her until she was dry. He organized an egg and a seed cooperative, and hosted informal gatherings when neighboring farmers shared farming tips and stories. He offered seminars on chicken coops, fertilizers, soil conservation, hybrid seeds, and new farm machinery, and these seminars were attended by blacks and whites alike.

Although most of the white farmers stopped coming after a while, none seemed to mind that Jordan offered instruction for his black neighbors. Jordan never intended for Koinonia Farm to be a center of civil rights organizing, and it never was.

But he also never thought of the farm as an experiment intended to promote integration, even though the Jordans were intentional in their commitment to interracialism. Jordan rather imagined Koinonia Farm as a place of Christian fellowship whose members seek to practice "the Way of Jesus" in their daily life and work. Jordan also repeatedly asserted Koinonia's "family principle" that there "be no favorite children, whether they are blondes or brunettes, white or black." Certainly the application of the teachings of Jesus Christ to southern society would have unsettling consequences for the status quo; but the means by which Jordan hoped to achieve reconciliation (a term he always preferred to integration) would be wholly theological. Reconciliation was first and foremost a quality of life in the Body of Christ, a requirement of citizenship in the kingdom of God. And, as he saw it, life in the Body of Christ from the perspective of Sumter

County, Georgia, involved three interconnected passions: the practice of nonviolence as the moral disposition of the Gospel; the preservation, cultivation and protection of the soil, "God's holy earth"; and the proclamation and provision of hope to the "those who suffer and are oppressed."

The community evolved without clear design or direction. In the next few years, only a dozen or so men and women moved to the farm; most were like-minded Christians from southern Baptist or Anabaptist traditions. Other people came for short visits—college students, volunteers from the Mennonite Central Committee, and a handful of Baptist radicals like Will D. Campbell and Foy Valentine. Still, as far as racial reconciliation was concerned, Koinonia was all dressed up with no place to go. And as the Jordans discovered when they moved into their dilapidated farmhouse, it wasn't even dressed up.

Having survived the boycotts, the harassments, and the investigations, the Koinonians began the new decade of the sixties uncertain of the future and of what their mission in the changing South would be. Jordan never intended Koinonia Farm to be anything more than a "demonstration plot of the Kingdom of God," a living parable of reconciliation, although he never had a clear picture either of how a Christian community of total sharing and racial equality would transform the social order. Where should Koinonia Farm go from here?

The Psalmist had spoken of "waiting on God," of dwelling in the house of the Lord and gazing quietly upon the beauty of the Lord. As it turned out, in the period of uncertainty following the years of boycotts and violence, Koinonia Farm was given the grace to do nothing. Jordan's theological influence was the nineteenth century Swiss pastor and social reformer, Christoph Blumhardt, who liked to say that in times of uncertainty, God teaches his children lessons in waiting and abiding in the truth. Blumhardt was a man of enormous energy fully engaged in the social challenges of his day; yet he always made clear that the kind of moral action most energizing to the kingdom of God was the kind that emerges from a disciplined waiting. "Get busy and wait," he said. There is "action in waiting."

What was Koinonia to do next?

Out of the long season of attacks and harassment, and despite the attrition and confusion that followed, Jordan and the remaining Koinonians were to be surprised by an infusion of new energy.

In 1961, a young black pastor from Petersburg, Virginia, named Charles Sherrod moved into a poor neighborhood in nearby Albany,

Georgia. Sherrod had come as an organizer with the newly formed Student Nonviolent Coordinating Committee (SNCC), and he had come with the purpose of getting to know his neighbors and learning the needs of the community. Jordan was impressed with Sherrod, especially by his respect for place, his attention to the grassroots and his commitment to living among the people one serves. Sherrod, like most SNCC activists, was full of admiration for Martin Luther King and came to the movement as a result of his leadership. But also like most SNCC workers, Sherrod had become uneasy with SCLC's top-down approach to racial organizing. Decisions about local protests tended increasingly to be made by a small circle of advisors. Through Sherrod and other young activists moving into southwest Georgia, Jordan rediscovered many of the same beliefs and convictions that had animated Koinonia's mission in the early days: the respect for particular communities, living with the poor, concern for economic development, and attunement to the local story.

A remarkable thing happened. From 1962 to 1965, Koinoina Farm found itself reborn as a place of hospitality for movement activists, peacemakers and southern dissidents. SNCC workers in southwest Georgia came for Bible studies and prayer meetings with Jordan and the Koinonians but also held organizing and training sessions on the farm, seminars on nonviolence, voter registration meetings, literacy schools and citizenship workshops; scores of "ministers, priests, rabbis and lawyers" stopped by as well for a meal, a shower and a night's sleep, and sometimes stayed longer. "On Sundays I used to go out there and talk to Clarence and meditate," recalled SNCC's Sherrod, "and it was just nice to be on a farm and be quiet." Some years as many as a thousand men and women came to the farm for retreat and fellowship. Among them were CORE staff members who found friends in the Koinonians and helped tend the vineyard; as well as pacifists of all stripes who offered each other help filing their applications for Conscientious Objector status or mustering up the courage to face jail; and back-to-nature-types who came for the simple life. In all of this, Koinonia Farm's contribution to the movement was essential, if not easily discerned. A young activist said, "Koinonia was my haven because it if hadn't have been for Clarence, I don't know whether I would have been able to exist."

Burnout is the activist's occupational hazard, yet little attention has been given to the role of retreat in the movement story. The Koinonia story has been ignored in our telling of the civil rights movement because of the difficulty of appreciating the importance of contemplative and moral discipline in social protest. Koinonia makes nothing happen in terms of a familiar statistical-legal measure. Yet the movement in the South, like Bonhoeffer's resistance movement in Germany and Gandhi's satyagraha in India, depended on intentional communities dedicated to work, study, and contemplation. "A life of hospitality is much less about dramatic gestures than it is about steady work," the theologian Christine Pohl has written, about "faithful labor that is undergirded by prayer and sustained by grace." Koinonia might be best described as a vital part of the health of the movement, where weary men and women found refreshment and restorative fellowship between the major campaigns.

Jordan proclaimed the message of the "God Movement." "There must be a greater and deeper movement than the civil rights movement," he said, "the God Movement, the stirring of His mighty Spirit of love, peace, humility, forgiveness, joy and reconciliation in the hearts of all of us. Maybe it's just a dream . . . but the only alternative that I can see to the dream is a nightmare." Jordan began translating the Greek New Testament term *basileia* as "movement" rather than "kingdom," as "something that gets underway spontaneously"—a "New Order," "Spiritual Order," "Kingdom Movement," "Spiritual Movement," and "Spiritual Family." The God Movement is not something you enter into and flop down and say, "God, I made it." The God Movement is rather like the day of the Sabbath, not in a sense of rest or withdrawal from action but in the sense of harmony and tremendous activity concentrated in the task at hand, "activity coordinated with God's purposes." In short, Jordan's God Movement was the new social order that bursts into being in the life and teachings of Jesus. Jesus had founded the most revolutionary movement in human history: a movement built on the unconditional love of God for the world and the mandate to love likewise. Jordan wrote to peaceworker Craig Peters: "I am increasingly convinced that Jesus thought of his messages as not dead-ending in a static institution but as a mighty flow of spirit which would penetrate every nook and cranny of man's personal and social life . . . I really don't think we can ever renew the church until we stop thinking of it as an institution and start thinking of it as a movement."

Preaching the God Movement circa 1965 carried with it inevitable criticisms of the civil rights movement. Jordan asked the question: Has the civil rights movement mistaken its demand for equal rights as the fulfillment of the search for beloved community? Has the movement lost sight of the fact that the Christian always passes through the mortal world as sojourner, pilgrim and "stranger to the well-ordered communities of this earth?" Have movement leaders and participants failed to acknowledge that the affirmation they seek can only be conferred by God? Abiding by a different logic and motivation, and thus "set apart by God's spirit," the Christian, said Jordan, must remain a stranger amidst the violent and dehumanizing structures of the world. Jordan explained in a sermon: "[The Christian] is a stranger because his ideas are strange and foreign. He's a stranger because he's a new creature. His life is on new foundations. He's got new motivations, new valuations, a new outlook. He's a stranger in the council halls of the wicked . . . He isn't at home there. He has caught a vision of a world of sharing and he isn't at home in the halls of finance and big business. That's not his land . . . The real home of the Christian is this earth, under the spirit and guidance and influence of Jesus Christ."

In other words, the civil rights movement might have succeeded in changing the laws of the South and nation, but if it secured these changes by compromising its redemptive mission, it was a failure.

What would Jordan have King do? King would do his own soul and the movement's well by going to the wilderness and making retreat, regathering his spiritual and moral energies, rekindling his affection and loyalty to Coretta, and rebuilding his relationship with his daughter Yokie, and his two sons, Dexter and Martin, living now in an Atlanta netherworld of nannies and tutors like fatherless children. He should seek to live singlemindedly in a community and demonstrate in a local environment the truth and meaning of his cosmic peregrinations. King should not consider himself exempt from the ordinary demands of the Christian life: walking humbly, "rooted and built up in him," as the apostle Paul wrote, "clothed with humility," "sober," "vigilant," "subject one to another."

Perhaps, but King had led the Montgomery movement on the foundations of the black resistance church. With so secure a foundation, King, unlike the Southern Baptist Jordan, felt no ambivalence in engaging and reforming the civic and political realm. As a result, the "spiritual struggle" in Montgomery had included both the church and the world in its scope; the church's politics demanded action in both fields. Any affirmation of racial unity that did not require material change was cheap, and it was not an appropriate Christian response. One need only observe the Gnostic arrangements of white evangelical Christendom, its preference for the spirit over the harsh judgments of the body, especially when the black body was on its feet in social protest. But the black church was everywhere in Montgomery, on the streets, in the cars, overflowing onto the sidewalk, and as a result there was no need to worry about politicizing the parish. Legal and social reform was essential to the movement.

Still, Jordan's criticism that the civil rights movement had failed to stay the course on redemption and reconciliation in the South paled in comparison to his unforgiving judgments on southern evangelicalism, the heartbreaking calumny, indeed the heresy, of the white church in the South. Jordan's denunciation of the southern church in his final sermons is harder than any King's had ever been. (It would not be until the late 1960s and the writings of radical black theologians such as Vincent Harding and James Cone that denunciations of the white church appeared with similar fury and power.)

King had largely assumed the role of spiritual counselor to an erring white church, which stood in need of instruction. In his "Letter from the Birmingham City Jail," he described his "deep disappointment" with the white church. "I have wept over the laxity of the church," he said. "Yes, I see the church as the Body of Christ. But, oh! How we have blemished and scarred that body through social neglect and fear of being nonconformists." The judgment of God is upon the church as never before, he allows, but as the forfeiture of the church's authenticity and relevance. His tears are "tears of love."

But Clarence Jordan asserted with prophetic wrath that the southern church had been overtaken by "false prophets" who would be "chopped down and thrown into the fire." The righteous man sheds no tears for the apostate church. Jordan read scripture with the passion of an old school fundamentalist, except he refused to demythologize reconciliation so as to save his hide. Jordan believed that born-again faith, if followed through to the end, if genuine, could not but transform white supremacy from the inside out. The process of transformation is set in motion, "when we receive Jesus, when we open our hearts to him and let him come in, bringing with him all his queer ideas about loving everybody, even one's enemies, about racial equality, about complete economic sharing, about humility." Racial reconciliation, economic redistribution, and prophetic pacifism are fruits of the spirit, the gifts of Pentecost. Jordan's born-again social radicalism stood as evidence that when the fruits are absent, so was salvation. The southern sanctuary was the construction of apostates and atheists.

"Here is what I am trying to say," he told an interviewer towards the end. "If the barriers that divide man, and cause wars, race conflict, economic competition, class struggles, labor disputes are ever to be broken down, they must be broken down in small groups of people living side by side, who plan consciously and deliberately to find a way wherein they can all contribute to the Kingdom according to their respective abilities."

Koinonia Farm is best remembered as an exercise in repentance, reconciliation and costly discipleship—not as a solution to the race problem. To be sure, Jordan's lessons were not lost on a younger generation of civil rights workers, including Charles Sherrod, who understood that "much of the spade work" of SNCC's organizing in southwest Georgia "has already been done by the Koinoina farm people . . . even if it is emblazoned with bullet fringes," and even if the community "could have gone a lot farther than it did." Still, in another sense, Koinonia went further than SNCC, for while the civil rights movement defeated segregation and forever changed American society, of repentance, reconciliation and costly discipleship the nation has experienced precious little. Jordan's alternative theological vision of South required a quieter revolution.

In the end, the civil rights movement and the God movement illuminate two trajectories of building beloved community which diverge and sometimes turn against the other: the church as the agent of social empowerment and the Christian community as a distinctive social reality that repudiates secular power.

These two visions are not mutually exclusive; they overlap at times and coexist in complex ways relative to the social situation. Yet as these trajectories form an arch from Montgomery through Sumter County into subsequent decades of congregational activism they forge differing visions and hopes of Beloved Community. Charles Sherrod summarized one of the basic differences: "The Koinonians didn't believe in any suing people. We were nonviolent but we believed in suing the hell [out] of somebody if we could, especially when they left us without jobs." Although there was a small degree of white involvement in Montgomery, as there was some degree of black involvement in Koinonia, the work of reconciliation did not offer the satisfactions of political organizing. Reconciliation's success was difficult to measure, and there seemed to be no end to the complexity of its conditions and demands. Reconciliation and beloved community would always be experienced as broken and incomplete, as an eschatological reality. Jordan explained in a 1966 letter to his son, "This is what always baffles me—Koinonia is forever dying and forever living. We should have conked out long ago, but somehow others come in the nick of time. This half-born condition is agonizing, and I could wish it otherwise, but there it is."

Jordan died suddenly on a cold and clear afternoon in late October of 1969. He had been working in his one-room writing shack in the cornfield, where he had recently completed his *Cotton Patch Gospel of Matthew*. The county coroner refused to come to the farm to issue a death certificate; so the dead body of the preacher was driven into Americus in the back of a station wagon. Jordan was buried the next afternoon in a cedar coffin wearing blue jeans. The service bore the familiar evidence of a prophet never honored in his home as white clergy and churchgoers from Americus ignored the occasion. But when the coffin was lowered into the red ground, the two-year-old daughter of Millard and Linda Fuller, who had recently joined the Koinonia community and would soon establish Habitat for Humanity, began singing the only song she knew by heart:

> Happy birthday to you;
> Happy birthday to you;
> Happy birthday, dear Clarence;
> Happy birthday to you.

7

"Loving Respect, Clear Disagreement"

Vincent Harding interviewed by John Pierce

Martin Luther King, Jr. and Clarence Jordan used different means toward the same end: racial equality.

King orchestrated mass boycotts to cripple economic systems and raise awareness of the injustices against African Americans. Jordan suffered the brunt of boycotts launched against his interracial farming community in southwest Georgia—along with direct acts of violence.

At Jordan's request, mutual friend Vincent Harding brought the two together in Albany, Georgia, in 1961 to discuss their different perspectives.

Surprisingly, this quiet but spirited meeting of two Georgia-born Baptists—with strong devotion to breaking down human barriers of discrimination—has remained little known. But Harding recalled that meeting and other events from the Southern freedom movement in a March interview with *Baptists Today* at the Atlanta University Center.

Headed South

A careful historian, Harding recalls the events going back more than a half-century with caution but surprising clarity. At age eighty-one, he confesses that some of things he witnessed and some events he has written about over the years may blend together.

But a memorable trip from Chicago to the South in 1958—in which he first met King and Jordan, separately—is quite clear.

While studying at the University of Chicago, Harding was part of a pastoral team in the "experimental, interracial" Woodlawn Mennonite Church—where bright, young, and idealistic members liked to talk about the struggle for racial equality. They were mostly students or recent graduates of the University of Chicago or the Mennonite Biblical Seminary.

Eventually, the conversation shifted to: "Why do we keep talking about this? Maybe some of us should just see what happens if we did this in the South."

Harding described himself and his peers as "kind of crazy anyway." So five young men—three white, two black—piled into an old station wagon and headed for Little Rock, where desegregation battles had made the news.

Some might call them an early version of "freedom riders," said Harding. But "Christian riders" would be more fitting, he said, as their faith in Christ clearly drove their mission.

After moving through Arkansas and Mississippi, the young men headed for southern Alabama to a Mennonite camp. Finding interracial housing in the South at that time was very difficult.

Bedside Meeting

None of the five had ever met King, though Harding recalled having heard the rising civil rights leader speak to a large gathering in Chicago. But on this September day in 1958, they decided to give it a try.

"It didn't make sense to be on our kind of journey, to be in Alabama and not try to make contact with him," Harding recalled his band of brothers thinking.

To his surprise, a bank of phone books in Mobile had the phone number listed for the pastor's home in Montgomery. Coretta Scott King answered the telephone call.

"Martin had been stabbed by a deranged woman in Harlem on a book-signing tour," said Harding, an event that hadn't registered with him at the time of his call. "He had gone home to recover."

Coretta said she was uncertain if Martin would be able to meet with them, but for them to come on by. So they drove to Montgomery.

Upon their arrival, Coretta went back to the bedroom to tell her husband about the young Mennonites. She reported back that "he'd be very glad to see you." With King in his pajamas and robe, the five young men from Chicago gathered chairs around his bed and made a "wonderful first connection."

Harding recalled being impressed by King's "tremendous sense of humor."

"He kept congratulating us on the great feat of being able to get through Mississippi alive."

Harding said they talked about what King was trying to do in Montgomery and what they were trying to do in Chicago. They asked King about his hope for the South as a whole.

After about two hours, the men were leaving when King looked at Harding and his friend Ed Riddick and said: "You guys are Mennonites; you know about this matter of nonviolence. We need you. You ought to come down here and work with us sometime."

On To Koinonia

Clarence Jordan's interracial and controversial farm outside of Americus, Georgia, was a certain destination for the wandering Mennonites—though Harding doesn't recall how they first learned of Koinonia Farm.

"Clarence and Koinonia represented the same kind of commitment to Christian brotherhood and sisterhood—and we would find a welcome place there," said Harding.

So they pointed the station wagon toward southwest Georgia.

"Sometime after we left Montgomery, it may have been our next stop ... we got to Koinonia and got to meet Clarence," said Harding. "As you can imagine, we had many wonderful conversations."

Also memorable, Harding said, was being assigned for boarding to a house near the entrance to Koinonia—where evidence of bullets having been fired into the house remained on the wall just above his bed.

For Harding, that initial visit in 1958 "was the beginning of a long relationship with Clarence and Koinonia."

Off To Atlanta

A couple of years after his Southern adventure with friends, Harding and his new bride Rosemarie moved in Atlanta as representatives of the Mennonite Service Committee. With the Georgia capital as their base, they would travel all over the South and relate to a variety of individuals and organizations to further the cause of freedom.

Their commitment, said Harding, was to find "where the way of love can take us in the midst of social struggle."

A real estate agent helped them find a twelve-room residence that would become the Mennonite House in which the Hardings would provide hospitality and out of which they would carry forward their mission. Unknown to them at the time, Martin and Coretta King (who by then had moved to Atlanta) lived just around the corner. Their friendships with the Kings subsequently grew.

Harding said King asked the young Mennonite couple to help in various efforts of the freedom movement. Two specific requests were to be involved in nonviolence training and to identify white persons who were sympathetic to the freedom cause but might fear making direct contact with King or local movements. Desegregation efforts in Albany, Georgia, were of particular interest at that time.

So Vincent and Rosemarie gladly took the charge whereby a "strange black Mennonite couple" would talk with white Southerners "especially on the grounds of their Christian faith"—and encourage them to take a stand based on faith rather than politics.

Harding said the struggle was "not just the cause of black people, but the cause of justice and democracy—and, of course, the cause of a Christian way of life."

More Clarence

"Whenever we were operating in south Georgia, we wanted to spend some time with Clarence at Koinonia," said Harding, who often took Mennonite House groups down to the Farm for visits as well.

So before going to Albany to build the local support that King had requested, the Hardings went to Koinonia. Clarence expressed concerns about the strategy of using boycotts against stores and institutions that would not open their doors to African Americans.

"As Clarence talked with Rose and me, he asked if there was any way in which we could arrange for him and Martin to talk together about his hesitations—growing, for one thing, out of his own experience there at Koinonia with boycott as a weapon."

Harding said Jordan knew firsthand of the capacity of boycotts to do harm and he didn't think such actions were consistent with Jesus' call to love your enemies and not return evil for evil. So Harding promised Jordan that he would try to bring the two together to discuss his concerns.

"I knew that Martin would be very glad to meet Clarence in light of Clarence's own history," said Harding. "Both of them were Baptists; they had much in common."

Albany Meeting

Things were heating up in Albany when King arrived in December 1961. He didn't have time to go to Koinonia, but asked if Jordan might come to Albany, Harding recalled.

Clarence and Koinonia partner Con Browne were welcomed to the Albany home of physician and civil rights leader W. G. Anderson to meet with King. The mutual affection was obvious, said Harding, describing both King and Jordan as "full of grace."

Yet "Clarence quickly moved to the direct concern that he had," said Harding.

While he doesn't recall the full conversation in detail, Harding said King listened intently and said he understood Jordan's concerns. However, King felt that the use of nonviolent protest and boycotts was a right and effective strategy.

"They engaged each other with loving respect and clear disagreement," said Harding. "For those things to go together is a great gift."

Harding said he does not believe his two friends ever met again, but that Koinonia opened its community often to others working in the Albany movement.

Compare, Contrast

King and Jordan had similarities and differences, said their mutual friend. "Both had developed a really impressive capacity to listen."

By the time they met in Albany in 1961, King had become a world-known figure, said Harding, and had much experience communicating in public and with the media. Jordan's work—as a writer and teacher—was done more quietly.

The two, he said, were "operating on absolutely different scales." Yet, both ministries were needed, he added—intimate relationships and work within the larger community.

"They both enjoyed people," said Harding. But as King's fame grew, casual relationships became more difficult due to "people wanting to get a piece of him."

Both of his friends shared a tremendous sense of humor, said Harding, although Jordan's was better known.

"Clarence was probably more of a storyteller," said Harding, who quickly added that King had gifts in that area as well.

Harding said he finds it fascinating that both were Georgians and Baptists—with roots in their native South where storytelling is common.

Christian Disciples

In the early 1960s, when Harding moved to the South, he discovered that the term Southerner "only meant white people." But some African Americans in the movement—Julian Bond being one of the first, he recalled—began to identify themselves in that way, said Harding.

Southern roots and Baptist upbringings are not what Harding remembers most about the commonality shared by his two friends, however.

"They both were men who took Jesus absolutely seriously," said Harding. "That was obviously one of the major grounds on which they could stand for their conversation. They both were convinced that the path of discipleship was their path and that was the way they wanted to go."

And their disagreements over methodologies, the noted historian added, fit well within the great tradition of Christian disciples since the time of Christ.

The two Baptists of the South with deep Christian commitments to the value of all persons—and a willingness to risk their lives for such a cause—died a year and a half apart: King from an assassin's bullet at age thirty-nine in April, 1968, and Jordan from a heart attack at age fifty-seven in October, 1969.

Yet their witnesses still bear light—and their shared mission continues.

8

Spittin' Image of the Almighty

Joyce Hollyday

The Scripture text a few months before was the story of Jonah and the whale. Circle of Mercy, the faith community in Asheville, North Carolina, that I co-pastor, gathers on Sunday nights. So the tale was still vividly planted in the minds of the three-year-old triplet boys, who are part of our congregation, when their parents were getting them ready for bed that night.

"I'm Jonah!" declared Will proudly, as his mother wrestled him into his pajamas.

"*I'm* the big fish!" piped up Connor, puffing out his cheeks and spreading his arms wide.

Jack's little shoulders slumped, and a crestfallen look overtook his face, as he sighed sadly, "I guess *I* have to be *God*."

In the story as Jack heard it, Jonah was a superhero, the big fish was... well, a big fish. And God was a disembodied voice behind the scenes with a bit part.

If there's anything that Clarence Jordan wanted us to know without a doubt, it's that Jack had it wrong. Through the founding of the Koinonia community, through his Cotton Patch version of the Scriptures, and through the witness of his life, Clarence reminded us over and over that

God took on flesh, entered into the world and all its pain, and continues to be actively at work among us.

In his introduction to *The Cotton Patch Version of Luke and Acts*, Clarence wrote: "Jesus has been so zealously worshipped, his deity so vehemently affirmed, his halo so brightly illumined, and his cross so beautifully polished that in the minds of many he no longer exists as a man. He has become an exquisite celestial being who momentarily and mistakenly lapsed into a painful involvement in the human scene, and then quite properly returned to his heavenly habitat. By thus glorifying him we more effectively rid ourselves of him than did those who tried to do so by crudely crucifying him."

Clarence's unique Cotton Patch translation of the Scriptures took Jesus out of his historical context and set him down in modern Georgia: being born in Gainesville and placed in an apple crate; confronting the leaders of the Southern Baptist Convention in Atlanta; dying by lynching. Clarence wanted to emphasize the humanity of Jesus, the Incarnation, the Word Become Flesh that walked the earth and was a full participant in the sorrows and joys of life.

He also wanted his readers to have a sense of participation in the Scriptures, rather than the feeling of being spectators. He sought, in his words, "to restore the original feeling and excitement of the fast-breaking *news*—good news—rather than musty history."

That good news was announced nowhere more clearly than in Jesus' Sermon on the Mount, which Clarence called "the platform of the God Movement," whose purpose was "not to evoke inspiration but perspiration." Clarence wrote in his commentary about it that the Sermon, found in the fifth, sixth, and seventh chapters of the Gospel of Matthew, "is a mighty gushing stream from which we've only taken one or two drops . . . We are at a banquet table laden with bounties and we are doodlebugging around trying to decide if we want cream of wheat or cold cereal."

When preaching about it, Clarence often introduced the Sermon with the story of Jesus' temptation in the desert, from the fourth chapter of Matthew. He interpreted that story as Jesus' rejection of the three most powerful ideas that bid for people's minds and hearts: materialism, ecclesiasticism, and militarism. He saw conversion to Christ as a radical change in one's whole way of thinking and living, a shift in loyalties from the ways of the world to the principles of the God Movement. He understood that such a transformation wasn't easy; that it required an environment of nurture and connection.

In the fall of 1941, at a Fellowship of Reconciliation meeting in Louisville, Clarence had met a gentle missionary named Martin England. The two men shared a love for Scripture and a conviction about living according to the Sermon on the Mount, as well as a concern about the massive failure of farming during the Great Depression and the resultant throngs of people streaming into cities, facing overcrowding, substandard housing, and uncertain employment.

Clarence and Martin began to dream together. They eventually found a worn-out, eroded, virtually treeless 440-acre farm eight miles southwest of Americus, Georgia. Clarence proclaimed, "This is it." He named their experiment Koinonia, the Greek word appearing in the Acts of the Apostles that identified the early Jerusalem church, whose members pooled all their resources and shared the life of Jesus Christ in a spirit of compassion and reconciliation.

Twenty-four years after the community's founding, in a talk to an audience that was captured on tape, Clarence told the story of the leap of faith they took, punctuating his reflections with hearty laughter:

> When we started that thing, we were supposed to pay the fellow twenty-five hundred dollars down. And Martin England, who was a missionary under the American Baptist Foreign Mission Society to Burma—he and I agreed on the common purse—we were going to pool everything—and I had the idea Martin was loaded. I don't know why I should think that—[him] being an American Baptist missionary. But he talked "Let's do this" and "Let's do that," and I said, "Yeah, let's do," and I thought he had the money.
>
> So when we finally pooled our common assets, we had fifty-seven dollars and thirteen cents—and both of us had resigned our jobs. But on the first day of November 1942, right on the button, we walked in that real estate office and put down that twenty-five hundred dollars. A fellow brought it to us, said the Lord had sent him with it. I didn't question him, where he'd been talking to the Lord or anything like that. We'd take it right quick, before the Lord changed his mind.

The money had come from a Baptist businessman named Arthur Steilburg, who was attracted by Clarence's sincerity, idealism, and exuberance. When Clarence had shared with him the dream of Koinonia Farm, Arthur said that, when he made some money, he'd "put a few dollars into it." Early in 1942, he won a large contract with the Army to construct living quarters and storage buildings in Indiana. When he handed Clarence an envelope with his contribution a few months later, Clarence expected those "few dollars"—and was stunned to find the exact amount of the down payment.

Clarence ended his talk by comparing faith to walking up to an automatic door: "I don't know what opens it, but it does. I know you got to walk right into it to make it open. I've seen this happen time and again in our experience. We started with absolutely nothing, and I'm here to tell you we've been there twenty-four years and we've never missed a meal." He stopped and laughed, then added dryly, "We've had to postpone several."

When the Jordans and Englands bought the farm, the barn and tool shed sagged with age, several sections of fence were down, and the ancient farmhouse was uninhabitable. While Clarence and Martin made repairs, Mabel England and the three young Martin children, and Florence Jordan and the two Jordan children, stayed with family members elsewhere.

Clarence reported that he went up on the roof every morning to see what the neighbors were doing. When the neighbors plowed, he and Martin plowed; when the neighbors planted, they planted. The two men had to hitch each other to the plow to lay out rows for fruit and nut trees. Florence and Mabel and the children moved there in April 1943, when the house was, according to Florence, "at least campable."

The Koinonians launched into a highly successful poultry-and-egg business. A neighbor helped Clarence and Martin build a first-rate house for the chickens, causing Mabel to lament, "I begged them several times to put me in the new chicken house. It didn't leak, it was well heated, and it would seat two thousand!" They helped a number of farmers establish their own chicken flocks and set up an egg cooperative. Clarence designed the first mobile peanut harvester and instituted a "cow library," from which families in need of milk could check out a cow free of charge.

Life at Koinonia Farm was rigorous and disciplined—but with plenty of time for picnics and storytelling, for turning the grape harvest into wine and lying on the ground under an autumn sky while Clarence delivered lectures on the constellations. As Gene Singletary, who joined in 1948, described it, "It was kind of like a day-to-day invention."

Meetings went half the night while the members designed their life together. They had breakfast every morning before dawn, followed by Bible study, usually led by Clarence. He referred to the community not as a structure, but as a family, and he believed that no Christian witness was more distinctive than people living and working together, sharing all that they had, and caring for one another like sisters and brothers.

Clarence said that everyone entered the community in a common condition known as "flat broke." When a woman with sizable resources wanted to join, Clarence insisted that she give away her fortune first. He told her that otherwise she would constantly wonder if the community loved her for her money, or she would expect people to treat her like their guardian angel. Or, perhaps worst of all, Clarence said, "We'd quit growing peanuts and start discussing theology."

He understood well both the challenge and the blessedness of that condition of "flat broke." His Cotton Patch translation of the Gospel of Luke's rendering of Jesus' most important sermon begins: "The poor are God's people, because the God Movement is yours. You who are now hungering are God's people, because you will be filled. You who are now weeping are God's people, because you will laugh . . ." (Luke 6:20–23).

It ends this way: "But let me tell you something: Love your enemies, deal kindly with those who hate you, give your blessings to those who give you their cursing, pray for those insulting you . . . *You all*, love your enemies, and be kind, and lend, expecting nothing. And you'll get plenty of 'pay'; you'll be the spittin' image of the Almighty" (6:27).

This word about loving enemies may just be Jesus' most difficult command. We can be thankful that Clarence took it to heart—so few Christians have. On a summer day in 1933, as a college student enrolled in ROTC (Reserve Officers' Training Corps), just days from being commissioned as a second lieutenant in the US Cavalry, Clarence was galloping on a horse, pistol in one hand and saber in the other, stabbing and shooting at straw and cardboard dummies.

But the command "love your enemies" kept echoing in his mind. Before the drill was over, the Sermon on the Mount had urged Clarence off his mount. He resigned his commission and decided to become a preacher. And we are all the better for it.

When Koinonia was founded, the Second World War was raging, and several conscientious objectors found sanctuary at the farm. Rooted in the example of Jesus, the Koinonians' pacifism in that era of high patriotism was highly unpopular. But it was not nearly as troubling to their white neighbors as their views on race.

Clarence hired a local man, a former sharecropper, to help with the farming, and he joined the community at meals. Several white neighbors observed this violation of Southern tradition, and the Koinonia families waited for the hostility to come. They didn't have to wait long.

Late one afternoon, a menacing delegation arrived at the farm. The spokesman said to Clarence, "We're from the Ku Klux Klan, and we're here to tell you we don't allow the sun to set on anybody who eats with niggers." Clarence glanced over at the western sky and noticed that the sun was creeping low. He thought a bit and swallowed hard a few times.

Then he reached out, grabbed the man's hand, and started pumping away, saying, "Why, I'm a Baptist preacher and I just graduated from the Southern Baptist Seminary. I've heard about people who had power over the sun, but I never hoped to meet one." The man admitted to being the son of a Baptist preacher himself. They all laughed, and nobody noticed that the sun had slipped down below the horizon.

In that encounter, Clarence exhibited the unblinking courage and disarming wit that would become his trademarks. They stood him in good stead as he faced a regular onslaught in the years to come from bigots and hatemongers and preachers of false ideology—the ones he said possessed "sheepskins from wolf-schools."

Clarence admitted that Koinonia's breach of segregation customs could lead to frightening consequences: "We knew white men could disappear just like black men. It scared the hell out of us, but the alternative was not to do it, and that scared us more."

Several members of Koinonia joined Rehoboth Baptist Church, where Florence taught an adult Sunday school class and Clarence frequently led the singing and played his trumpet. In 1950 a student from India attended church with them, and his dark skin created a great stir in the congregation. Soon after, a delegation of men from the church came to the farm and pleaded with Clarence to keep everyone from Koinonia away.

Clarence handed a Bible to one of the men and said that he'd be happy to apologize to the church if they could show him his offense in Scripture. The deacon slammed it down and shouted, "Don't give me any of this Bible stuff!" Clarence replied, "I'm asking you to give it to me," and calmly suggested that if the man didn't believe in the Bible then perhaps he himself should get out of the Baptist church.

In a lengthy letter read during a congregational business meeting after church one Sunday, the board of deacons accused the Koinonia members of disrupting Rehoboth's spiritual unity and creating disturbances during services, and moved to withdraw fellowship from them. A tense pause followed the reading of the charges. Then Florence stood abruptly and said, "I move that the recommendations of the deacons be accepted as read."

When the stunned moderator called for a second to the motion, he was answered with total, confused silence. Finally a deacon, who said later that he thought he was going to faint, pulled himself together enough to mouth a second, and the vote was taken. About two-thirds of the congregation voted in favor of the motion, the rest either too dismayed to take a stand or refusing to side with Florence. By what she would tell Clarence was the leading of the Spirit, Florence had effectively pleaded guilty to the charges, but also placed the congregants in the position of having to agree with her motion if they wanted to be rid of the Koinonians. And agreeing with Florence was something none of the congregants wanted to do.

A decade after it was founded, Koinonia Farm had grown to nineteen adults and twenty-two children, including four Jordan children. The year 1954 struck with a severe drought and heavy economic losses for the farm. But suffering more vast and vicious lay ahead. That year the US Supreme Court voted its landmark decision to desegregate schools. In reaction, White Citizens Councils and States Rights Councils sprouted up across the South. The one in Sumter County, Georgia, was formed with the express purpose of driving out Koinonia.

Early in 1956, Clarence tried to assist two African American students in their application to a formerly segregated business college in Atlanta. That was the spark that ignited an explosion of hostility. It began with threatening phone calls, grew to vandalism, and finally escalated into life-threatening violence. Fences were cut, crops stolen from the fields, and garbage dumped on the property. A truck's engine was ruined by sugar dumped in its gas tank, and nearly 300 fruit trees were chopped to the ground. The farm had its property insurance canceled.

On July 26, dynamite tore through Koinonia's roadside market, ripping off a section of the roof and destroying refrigeration equipment. Five days later, the Koinonians published an open letter in the local paper, explaining their principles and commitment to nonviolence, and welcoming visitors. It was met with a boycott of all Koinonia products and a coordinated refusal to sell to the farm the fertilizer, seeds, and gas it needed.

The day after Christmas, night riders sprayed bullets into the farm's gas pump, and on New Year's Day 1957 they aimed toward its homes and ripped down the sign at the entrance with bullets. For ten days, all day long, Koinonia's members met to hear everyone's feelings about whether to stay or to relocate. They raised concerns about their children's safety. Friends tried to convince them to move. But in the end, they decided to stay. Florence said, "We knew we wouldn't be the first Christians to die, and we wouldn't be the last."

Clarence spoke of the people around the farm "with their personalities twisted and warped by prejudice and hate . . . If there is any balm in Gilead; if there is any healing in God's wings; if there is any hope—shall we go off and leave people without hope? We have too many enemies to leave them . . . If it costs us our lives, if we must be hung on a cross to redeem our brothers and sisters in the flesh, so let it be. It will be well worth it. To move away would be to deny the redemptive processes of God."

On January 14 the roadside market was bombed again, completely demolished this time. More than a hundred smoked hams and other meats were ruined. No trace remained of large quantities of pecans, peanuts, honey, and eggs. When Clarence arrived on the scene, the grass around the market was on fire, threatening the beehives nearby. None of the forty or so gawking spectators, including law officers, made a move to help him put out the blaze.

Not long after that night, Clarence wrote a letter to his friend G. McLeod Bryan:

> When we came over a hill we could see the fiery glow on the horizon, and this ignited a burning in my heart. I was scorched with anger, and I'm sure if I had known who had committed the act, there would have been considerable hatred in my heart . . . But as I had occasion to think, I realized that the hate was rooted in a consuming possessiveness. True, I had given up personal possessions, only to find that I had transplanted it from an individual to a group basis. The market was our property; together we sweated to build it; and now it was burning, and I was too. The damned culprits have destroyed our property, I thought. And I hated their guts. Later I had the same reaction when various ones, including myself and my children, were shot at. The so-and-so's were trying to take our lives from us!
>
> The solution to this soul-destroying condition came only upon the recognition that neither property nor lives were ours but God's. They never had really been ours in any sense of the word. We hadn't even "given them back to Him"—they were His all along. And if this was the way He wanted to spend His property and His people in order to accomplish His purposes, why should we pitch a tantrum?

The attacks escalated, and the Koinonians set up a night watch—rotating teams of two people each, armed with flashlights, stationed in a car at the entrance to the farm. Night riders sprayed the car with machine gun fire, and tracer bullets streaked toward the homes and set a curtain on fire. A bullet ripped through a visitor's hat on a bedside stand. Guns were fired at the volleyball court where the children were playing, sending them screaming into a nearby orchard. A passing car fired on Clarence while he was on a tractor, and a rifle bullet barely missed 11-year-old Lora Ruth Browne in her family's home.

At a Ku Klux Klan rally, 150 men and women from all over southern Georgia donned their robes and hoods at the Americus fairgrounds. They ended their meeting with a motorcade to Koinonia, where they burned crosses.

Daring kindred souls from around the country arrived to offer their support and solidarity. Tennessee Baptist pastor Will Campbell, renowned for his racial reconciliation work, made a visit, along with the director of the Christian Life Commission of the Southern Baptist Convention, A. C. Miller, whom Will described as "a rotund and saintly man." Years later, Will recounted the discussion that went on between them about which one would sleep next to the window and which one against the far wall. The window had been drilled with rifle fire a few nights before, and A. C. Miller insisted that he should sleep by it, since he was an old man and Will was young. Will protested—but less than enthusiastically, he confessed later.

Clarence came in and settled the matter. He ran his hand over the outline of A. C.'s barrel-like belly, then motioned toward Will's. He said, "Now look. If a bullet comes through that window and A. C. is sleeping closest to it, it'll puncture his gut and Will won't be hurt. But if Will is closest to the window, it'll go right over him and get A. C. anyhow. Now, as near as I can figure it, that's the situation. So you boys go to sleep."

Friends around the country also provided aid in the form of financial pledges to cover Koinonia's lost insurance. Supporters signed promissory notes, pledging up to fifty dollars in the event of major damage to Koinonia property. Almost two thousand people participated in the effort.

That spring, a grand jury was convened to investigate Koinonia. No indictments were brought, but a sixteen-page report, published widely, accused Koinonia of being a communist front and of committing the acts of violence against itself, bombing its own roadside market to get attention and to collect insurance money. Clarence pointed out the absurd irony of being accused both of being a haven for conscientious objectors who didn't believe in violence, and of following the violent line of communism.

Charges of being communist or harboring communists became commonplace against the community. On one occasion, an accuser told Clarence that he was sure that recent visitors to Koinonia were communists and that Clarence therefore must be, too. Clarence looked him in the eye, gave the man his best smile, and said, "Why, being around those people doesn't make me any more a communist than being with you makes me a jackass."

The boycott continued its strangulation of Koinonia. The community members decided that their economic salvation might come through a mail-order business. With the slogan "Help us get the nuts out of Georgia," they called on friends around the country to finance, promote, and buy their pecans and pecan products.

The business, which still thrives today, brought economic relief but not an end to the harassment. Vandals sprinkled bags of pecans with turpentine. Koinonia member Con Browne was beaten at the railway express office while trying to send out a shipment. He was arrested, put in jail, and charged with beating himself up in order to get sympathy from passersby.

But other new ideas and people were on their way to Koinonia. Millard Fuller, a highly successful attorney and businessman, appeared at the farm one day. He planned to visit for two hours and instead stayed a month, declaring that his conversations with Clarence about being a Christian were "like a year, or two years, of seminary."

He and Clarence collaborated on the Fund for Humanity, which provided a way for low-income families to purchase land and build homes. Clarence envisioned one million acres of land for the poor. The two men began by marking off forty-two half-acre homesites on the edge of the farm's property, clustered around a playground. The experiment evolved into the renowned Habitat for Humanity and Fuller Center for Housing, which today provide affordable housing around the globe.

A decade ago, when I was at Koinonia doing research for *Clarence Jordan: Essential Writings*, a volume published by Orbis Books as part of its Spiritual Masters Series, I spoke with several of the neighbors who had been part of the community's early efforts. Standing on the porch at the farm that his grandfather had bought more than a hundred years before when he was freed from slavery, Carrenza Morgan and I surveyed the expanse of sunbaked red clay that stretched to the horizon, admiring vines hanging heavy with a harvest of muscadine grapes and breathing in summer air pungent with the smells of peanuts and pines.

Sixty years before, sharecropping and segregation were also part of this landscape, when a PhD-toting biblical scholar in overalls picked this corner of the world to launch a "demonstration plot" for the kingdom of God. He was called a troublemaker and a communist by some, a visionary and a saint by others. Everybody seemed to have an opinion about the tall preacher with a big mission, Clarence Jordan.

"When I get talking about Mr. Jordan, I can't help but just feel chills," said Mr. Morgan, whose wife had worked in Koinonia's baking kitchen for more than thirty years. "He meant so much to my life—and to so many more in this community. He believed that you were a human being, and he thought of civil rights as just treating people like you wanted to be treated. He treated you just like you were as white as he was. He was a God-sent man."

On a brisk October afternoon in 1969, sitting in his writing shack where he penned his Cotton Patch translations, Clarence Jordan succumbed to a heart attack. He was treated in death as in life—reviled by his enemies and tenderly loved by his family and friends. The coroner refused to come to the farm, so Millard Fuller drove Clarence's body to town in a station wagon. The body was placed in a cedar crate, of the kind used to ship fancy coffins, and a simple grave was dug in the hill where the community shared picnics.

As Clarence's body was lowered with ropes into the earth and the red Georgia clay was shoveled over it, Millard's then two-year-old daughter stepped up to the grave, looked down at the coffin of her friend, and sang a complete verse of "Happy Birthday, Dear Clarence" to him. Perhaps she had an understanding of the situation that escaped the adults around her. Maybe God placed the song in her heart. It is worth noting that her name was Faith.

A decade later, I made my first visit to Koinonia, to gather information for the first feature article I ever wrote for *Sojourners* magazine. The *Sojourners* staff was dedicating our annual December incarnation issue in 1979 to Clarence and Koinonia. In the last hour of that visit, I walked under a soft rain through the fields and past the pecan groves to Clarence's simple shack. Marked original manuscripts of sermons and Cotton Patch writings were on the shelves. A copy of a 1959 *Encyclopedia of Candy and Ice Cream Making* sat next to Clarence's worn Greek New Testament.

A blade of wheat, dried with age, lay on his tiny desk. I picked it up, wondering how it came to be there and how long it had rested in that place. It seemed appropriate to find it there. There is perhaps no better symbol for Clarence's life. "Unless a grain of wheat falls into the earth and dies, it remains alone; but if it dies, it bears much fruit."

Later, I went in search of a Cotton Patch version of the Gospel of John to find this verse from the twelfth chapter, hoping to draw some kernel of wisdom from Clarence's unique translation of it. I discovered that the manuscript of John was on his desk when he died; he had completed only the first eight chapters of the book. I felt cheated by the discovery—and by Clarence's early death at the age of 57. But what a generous and abundant life he lived; and what a rich legacy he left behind.

I dare say that when Clarence got to heaven, the Almighty saw as close to a spittin' image as one is likely to lay eyes on. Human in every way, Clarence was a witness to courage and compassion, to reconciliation and enemy love. He was a follower of Jesus who risked everything to live faithfully to the Gospel.

Among Clarence's statements most often quoted is this definition: "Faith is not belief in spite of the evidence but a life in scorn of the consequences." He spoke of fear as "the polio of the soul which prevents our walking by faith." Clarence Jordan learned to conquer his fears, to stare down hostile church members and boycotting neighbors and the guns of the Ku Klux Klan.

He liked preaching on the parable from Matthew 7:24–27, proclaiming that there are two types of Christians. The one who hears and *does* the Word of God is like a wise man who builds his house on a rock, with a foundation sturdy enough to survive through floods and wind. The person who hears the Word but doesn't do it, according to Clarence, is like the idiot who builds his house on sand, with a foundation that collapses in the storm with a terrible crash. He ended his sermons on the parable with the declaration, "Now let us go forth to classify ourselves." It's a challenge that stands for us today.

We once again—still—inhabit a time of division and misunderstanding, with escalating assaults on people of color and those who are impoverished. Exclusion and meanness are in the air. It is a time to pay close attention to Clarence and those like him who point us to a different way. For those who are tempted to give up hope, to feel powerless and overwhelmed, we can find inspiration in one who, to borrow his own phrase, "turned dreams into deeds." He gave us the sort of inspiration that leads to perspiration. And perseverance.

A few weeks before he died, a reporter asked Clarence, "When you get up to heaven and the Lord meets you and says, 'Clarence, I wonder if you could tell me in the next five minutes what you did down on earth,' what would you tell the Lord?" Without missing a beat, Clarence replied, "I'd tell the Lord to come back when he had more time." One wonders if the report has ended yet.

PART THREE
Community

9

Reflections on Florence Kroeger Jordan (1912–1987)

Linda Fuller Degelmann

The same year Koinonia celebrated its fortieth anniversary (1982), Florence celebrated her seventieth birthday. Five years later, in 1987, she would be called Home. Now, as we celebrate Koinonia's seventieth anniversary in 2012, we are honoring what would have been both Florence and Clarence's one-hundredth birthday.

First of all, I would like to share some personal reflections. Millard and I first met Florence and Clarence Jordan in December 1965. It was right after we had made a momentous decision to divest ourselves of our wealth and give it all away to worthwhile causes. We had felt God calling us to a life of Christian service but really didn't have a clue how to start. We, along with our two young children, had been to Florida and were headed back home to Montgomery when we decided to visit friends Al and Carol Henry. They had moved to Koinonia from Birmingham after being dismissed from a church because of Al's attempt to racially integrate the congregation. We intended to stay only an hour or two. Instead, we were so captivated by Clarence Jordan and the vibrant spirit of Christian community and hospitality that we asked if they had a place we could spend a few days. "Absolutely!" Clarence responded. "Stay as long as you like."

Clarence pointed to a small vacant house nearby and the four of us settled right in. Millard and I "earned our keep" by helping "ship the nuts out of Georgia" during that busy holiday season. The two-bedroom house had one unvented gas space heater, which we were instructed to turn off when we went to bed. I remember it didn't take long for the thermometer to drop in that small framed structure. This is when I first experienced Florence's thoughtfulness and generosity. She made sure we had plenty of blankets and then did something even more special. She made our children Chris and Kim flannel "pixie hats" that were pointed at the top and had ties to keep them snugly under their chins. They no longer had to bury their heads beneath the blankets to keep their ears warm. Instead, they could brighten their thoughts by pretending to be elves while drifting off to sleep.

Florence and I were together often during that phenomenal month. This is when I began to consider her a key mentor in my life. As we sat around munching roasted peanuts and popcorn in the evenings, Florence and Clarence told us some hair-raising stories about their encounters with local citizens, destruction of their roadside market *twice*, and the total boycott imposed by Americus businesses in the fifties. I had never met a woman, and few since, who practiced Christ's teachings without fear of the consequences. In a couple of years, God would call us back to Koinonia to work with the Jordans and other deeply committed Christians. This is when Florence and I got to know each other really well.

Florence Kroeger Jordan was born in Louisville, Kentucky on November 26, 1912—daughter of Ida Weilage and Fred F. Kroeger. She had brilliant blue eyes and grew tall and independent minded. Her father, an immigrant from Germany as a boy, became a successful businessman and one who had compassion for the poor.

Through her youth, she lived the city life. She was educated in public schools and attended Louisville Art Center after graduation from high school. She attended some classes at the University of Louisville and worked as an assistant to the librarian at Southern Baptist Theological Seminary. As Florence told it, "Clarence came into the library one day, looked over a number of books and then checked *me* out!"

In 1936, when Florence was twenty-four years of age, she became the wife of seminary graduate and Greek scholar Clarence Jordan. They remained in Louisville doing mission work the first few years of marriage. Then, as a true demonstration of courage, strength and commitment, Florence gladly followed her "farm-boy" and "preacher" husband to a rustic life in rural Georgia. Imagine no running water; meals cooked on a wood stove; clothes washed out of doors in a coal-heated iron pot. Over time, Florence and Clarence had four children: Eleanor, Jim, Jan, and Lenny—the latter two born at Koinonia. Actually, a third child was born at Koinonia but only lived a matter of days.

A woman of strength, Florence embraced difficulties and challenges. Often she would describe her life as "an adventure." In the Spring 1982 Koinonia newsletter, she was quoted as saying, "I don't think I'd be very happy with a 'normal' life." Perhaps one of the few "normal" things she did was take a week or two every year and visit family in Kentucky. Now and then, she traveled with Clarence on his speaking trips. Otherwise, she stayed put at "the farm" so as to provide stability to family and community.

While researching Florence's life, I found so much substantive and meaningful material that it was difficult to choose what to include and what to leave out. One of the most significant and obvious aspects to include was that Florence and Clarence were true partners in marriage, values, and vision throughout their thirty-three years together.

Clarence's endearing name for Florence was "Sweetheart" or simply "Sweet." When they had disagreements or conflicts as is common in any marriage, as far as I know, they kept them to the confines of their home. I never saw evidence otherwise. At times when Clarence spoke regarding Jesus' teachings on nonviolence, he would jokingly portray Florence in a way that would indicate she was anything but "sweet" and that she could take care of herself if the need arose.

At the end of one speech, Clarence called for questions. A gentleman stood up in the audience and in a deep voice asked, "Dr. Jordan, now it seems to me that you are taking Jesus' teachings on nonviolence a little too far. For instance, what if you were away on one of your speaking trips and someone broke into your house in the middle of the night. Wouldn't you want your wife to have a pistol so she could defend herself?"

Clarence responded, "That's an excellent question! Now let me make sure I understand what you are asking. You are posing a situation whereby an intruder enters my home when I am out of town ... right?"

"Yes, that's right."

"And, you are assuming that this intruder would be there to steal the contents of my house and perhaps even try to harm my wife and children?"

Again, the questioner responded, "Yes, that's right."

Clarence continued, "And, you are wondering how I feel about that very personal situation ... right?"

"Yes."

"Well, sir, upon reflecting on this very serious situation, I have to honestly respond that I would feel sorry for the intruder. You just don't know how strong my wife is! I believe that thief would turn on his heels and never think of returning."

Most of Florence's work at Koinonia centered on keeping accounts related to various enterprises such as crop, cattle, and poultry farming, the roadside market, and later, the pecan, fruitcake, and candy mail order business. Just like the other residents, she also took her turn cooking the daily communal noon meal, whether it was for the permanent residents or visitors.

Occasionally, a call would come in that a bus load of folks were on the way to visit the farm perhaps *that* evening or the next day. No problem for Florence. Ever since the Sumter County boycott that prevented Koinonia from selling or buying locally, Florence had gone forty miles to the south in Albany to do her shopping once a week. She would find the grocery store with the best price on turkeys and always keep several on hand in the freezer. By the time the group of visitors arrived, she would have pulled together a Thanksgiving feast with Koinonia residents providing a variety of side dishes.

Another story related to meals in the dining hall, and was captured in the June 1987 Koinonia newsletter. It said of Florence: "She's the only member of the Koinonia family with a regular seat at the lunch table—right by a west side window, facing into the dining hall. 'It's a good vantage point,' she explains, 'for spotting visitors and newcomers . . .' She would often invite them over for tea and some delectable homemade goodies . . ."

Lenny Jordan reminded me about one of his mother's pet peeves. "She hated flies." A hand-held fan was one of the ways Florence kept flies at bay while at the same time keeping cool. She had quite a collection of fans from which to choose . . . accordion or the stick variety. In addition to a fan, Florence usually had a cotton handkerchief or tissue handy for wiping her brow.

We have to assume that other than flies being a nuisance, her main concern was hygiene, since farm animals were nearby. Whether at home, the office, or the community dining room, she kept a fly swatter at the ready beside her chair. There was another reason she reached for her fly swatter . . . when her children got too rambunctious, prolonged arguing or did something naughty. Usually, all she had to do was bend slightly as if reaching for the swatter and that's all it took.

Florence insisted on children behaving themselves. She wouldn't hesitate to share with parents what she thought was unacceptable behavior.

DEGELMANN—*Reflections on Florence Kroeger Jordan (1912-1987)*

With four children, I experienced this personally. But she had her distinct way of showing kindness to children. She allowed children to knock on her door once each day—and only once—to receive a piece of candy. I witnessed this many times. Children would go alone and knock at Florence's door or several would go together. She took pleasure in allowing each child to look over the choices. She usually would chuckle or make some amusing comment about their selection. It was only a piece of candy, worth a penny or less, but it taught a lesson much more valuable: the joys that come from acts of kindness, giving and receiving.

On a deeper, spiritual level, take a look at these excerpts from "The Witness Was What Counted," an article Florence Jordan wrote for *Catholic Worker* magazine in 1983:

> What we were doing at Koinonia was preaching the end of the world—our neighbors' world... the end of the big plantation owners, the end of the man who'd sit on his porch and let somebody else do his work for little or no pay... This is where the problem comes—in the *incarnation* of the Word. It's not in the realm of ideas... There is only one question I'll ever have to answer, and that is have I been faithful? If a person is a maturing Christian at Koinonia, that's all we can ask. We all have to keep on growing.
>
> If you have a lot of rules and regulations, you begin to think that the rule is important. We feel that the leading by the Spirit is (what is) important.
>
> He (Clarence) told me that I'd never be the wife of a pastor at a First Baptist Church some place if I married him. He told me what he had in mind and I agreed with it. I knew I would end up probably on a farm in south Georgia without a whole lot of worldly goods.
>
> Christ was our authority and scripture was our authority and any one of us had to be equal under God... Of course, for us, that was a kind of a bold step because as Southerners we were "traitors" to our race and to our class... Jesus said love your enemies, and the church was blessing them (youth) to go out and kill... Churches were not doing that much sharing (with those in need). They were extremely segregated. So we felt that the Church was really not witnessing to three of the most important things Jesus (and the Apostle Paul) taught.
>
> We don't believe that community is for everyone... I've fallen flat on my face so many times... I was asked once what my theology was and I guess I only have one thing in my theology and that's *love*. I feel like that solves a lot of problems and answers a lot

of questions. If we're just able to love enough. Sometimes it's not easy. You might have a minimum of love for some people—but I do think you just have to have a lot of love and patience. And that love, of course, takes in the love of God, of Christ, and of your fellow human beings. Of course that's the first and great commandment. And the second is like unto it, love your neighbor as yourself.

According to the spring 1982 Koinonia newsletter, Florence was just as content at her typewriter writing articles, speeches, and letters to contributors as she was entertaining guests in her living room. When time would permit, she enjoyed reading. Florence could often be found puttering around her yard, tending to plants and flowers. Personally, I found her to be an excellent seamstress, who found it as much a necessity as she did a pleasure making most of her own clothes as well as some for Clarence and her children.

On Sunday afternoons, much the same as now, residents of Koinonia along with visitors and folks from the surrounding area gathered in the community dining hall for worship. Hymns were sung. Florence knew many from memory. One of her favorites:

> Great is Thy faithfulness!
> Morning by morning new mercies I see.
> All I have needed Thy hand hath provided.
> Great is Thy faithfulness, Lord, unto me.

One day, I noticed Florence walking on the rutted dirt road that ran behind her house between a pecan orchard and a large field of peanuts. She was wearing a bright red cape that I couldn't remember seeing previously. Like the rest of us, she dressed modestly. I realized she was headed to Picnic Hill to pay her beloved Clarence "a visit" near the spot he had been laid to rest in 1969. She didn't know then what we know now . . . that her life would endure eighteen years beyond Clarence's.

Upon her death, Florence was surrounded by family and friends as she was laid to rest beside Clarence . . . both in unmarked graves. She had hand-copied the poem "Immortality," which she had requested read at her burial.

DEGELMANN—*Reflections on Florence Kroeger Jordan (1912–1987)*

Immortality

Do not stand at my grave and weep . . .
I am not there. I do not sleep.
I am a thousand winds that blow,
I am the diamond glints on snow,
I am the sunlight on ripened grain,
I am the gentle autumn rain.

When you awake in the morning's hush,
I am the swift up flinging rush
Of quiet birds in circling flight.
I am the soft, star-shine at night.

Do not stand at my grave and cry . . .
I am not there. I did not die.

—Author unknown

Florence served faithfully in her roles as wife, parent, bookkeeper, nurturer, comforter, hostess, planner, fundraiser and pioneer. Some of her outstanding attributes could be defined as efficient, friendly, cheerful, generous, resourceful, loyal, trustworthy, and fearless. It goes without saying that there are other words and remembrances that can lend more glimpses into the life of Florence Jordan.

A few months following Florence's death, the September/October 1987 issue of a Southern Baptist publication stated, "Clarence died in 1969, leaving Florence as matriarch of the farm . . ." I asked the Jordan's youngest son Lenny Jordan what he thought about that and he responded that his mother didn't approve of the title, "Matriarch of Koinonia." I looked it up. The meaning of "matriarch" as found in Webster's Dictionary is "A female who rules or dominates her family and descendents." Some days her children may have thought that! However, when one considers Christian community as being bound by spirit rather than blood, Florence could very well fit the description as "a mother who is head of a family"—a family made up of thousands of people who ever stepped foot on Koinonia soil or supported the mission by any means.[1]

---

1. References: Jordan Family; Koinonia Archives (newsletters, speeches, articles, correspondence, photographs); Hargrett Rare Book, Manuscript and Collections Library of Georgia, University of Georgia, Athens; videotapte of Florence speaking to a class and town folk at Mercer University—Atlanta—about1982 (approx. 45 min.); Ancestry.com.

10

Memories of My Mother, Florence

JIM JORDAN

Thanksgiving was the Jordan reunion, but Christmas was when the Kroeger side of the family came to the forefront.

Florence came from a very, very close first and second generation German immigrant family. How close? Her cousins were all double first cousins as her mother's sister married her father's brother! And there were lots more family in the Louisville area. That may be overshadowed by the influence of the Talbotton Jordans.

We didn't have the opportunity to be very close to that side of the family as traveling to Louisville was by no means as easy as it is today. But Christmas was the time when Mother's European heritage of Christmas as a family celebration shone the brightest in a very special and unique way for us as children. Only later did we realize just how unique it was. Long before December she was thinking about making it a happy time for us. She taught us that Christmas was not about getting, but about the celebration. But she didn't want us to feel deprived, either. So, when she thought of or saw just the right little gift for one of us, it would go into her private "lay away" and later be a complete surprise. Or, more often than not it was a shirt, pajamas, or something like that, which she made while we were at school or asleep. At the same time she was teaching us to make gifts for each other. A couple of scraps of plywood and paint, together with some plastic cars from cereal boxes, made a toy garage and gas station for Lenny one year.

As the holiday season drew closer Mother would start planning and working on the foods that had always been a part of her childhood. Mother loved to bake Christmas cookies of all types. Her special cookie cutters would come out and there would be decorated sugar cookies in the form of Christmas trees, stars, angels, drummer boys, etc. More unusual were the traditional German cookies—Springerle, Pfeffernuss, Liebkuchen, each with its very distinctive aroma and flavor that I can evoke just thinking about it. She was baking fruit cake long before it became a farm industry. And then there was the Marzipan. She created miniatures of lots of things, but her favorites were fruits. Miniature bananas, apples, oranges, pineapples, complete with leaves and stems, all using the almond paste carefully and realistically colored with food coloring. As Eleanor was older she was allowed to team up in this artistic work. Mother managed to squeeze all this in around all her other work for the community. Often it was in the evening after everything else was done. I recall going to sleep to the smell of almond, anise, and other delicious flavors from cookies baking in the oven, all to be put away before we were up for breakfast.

Mother wasn't big on exercise and walking, but on the weekend before Christmas she led the family expedition out into the woods to find the perfect little pine to bring home and decorate as the Tannenbaum. Once on its stand, the prize collection of a handful of inherited ornaments that had been on her tree as a child would come out. We could help hang the ones that came from the ten cent store, but the old ones we didn't even think about touching.

Christmas morning for us was spent like most families, opening the presents, etc. But her big enjoyment was Christmas afternoon, when she had open house for everyone. The table was decorated with holly and candles and the special Yule treats she had spent so much of her time making. The tree stayed up until New Year's Day and through the holidays everyone was welcome to drop in for coffee, a glass of milk, and a Christmas cookie or two. Seeing everyone enjoy the treats she made was one of her few genuine pleasures. It was only later, too much later, that we really understood how she through love and determination left us with not only her genes but a part of her family heritage.

Christmas is the best example, but in reality it was a year round thing in smaller ways for Florence. She, more than anyone else, brought that old saying to life, "As children we were poor . . . but we didn't know it!"

11

Koinonia Co-founder Martin England— Insurance Guy

Dave Willis

During the fall of 2012, the Christian community in south Georgia and beyond celebrated the 100th anniversary of the birth of Clarence Jordan, co-founder of Koinonia Farm. The farm, which in 2008 received the Community of Christ International Peace Award, has been described as "the most daring social experiment in the South during the last century."

Jordan's involvement in the organization has been widely heralded—both before and after his death in 1969. His writings inspired a 1980s musical, *Cotton Patch Gospel*, and his work was recounted in a PBS documentary, *Briars in the Cotton Patch: The Story of Koinonia Farm*.

Lesser known is fellow co-founder Martin England. Even if they can't recall his name, readers of Tony Campolo's *Everything You've Heard is Wrong!* may be familiar with England, or at least his story. In addition to his formative role at Koinonia, England was instrumental in arranging a safety net that would ultimately provide for the family of Martin Luther King, Jr. following the civil rights leader's 1968 assassination.

In today's "red" and "blue" and "nothing in between" world, England would be typecast because of his profession. He was an insurance guy. But he was one that Campolo held up as an example to others. In the book, he explains that the Southern, white insurance agent was worried King lacked insurance that would take care of his family in case something happened to him.

"The determined salesman followed King for weeks, trying to tell the civil rights leader that he had a gigantic and urgent need," Campolo writes. "Finally, he got his opportunity. He sat Martin Luther King down, explained his need for life insurance, and got the necessary papers signed."

In 1990, I made my first connection—albeit a distant one—to Koinonia Farm. As a 30-something single guy, I took part in a Jimmy Carter Work Project in Tijuana, where I met Millard Fuller and David Snell. Fuller, of course, co-founded Habitat for Humanity with his wife Linda, as an outgrowth of Koinonia Farm. Snell headed up the Work Project, and today leads The Fuller Center for Housing, which he, Millard and Linda, and Ken Henson founded in 2005, based on the original biblical principles and methods developed at Koinonia.

While I may not have known of Clarence Jordan or Martin England at the time, I became wrapped up in the house-building effort their guiding principles spawned. I caught what Millard Fuller described as "Infectious Habititis." I worked alongside men, women, boys, and girls who shared a similar mission: to build in partnership with others to provide safe, decent, affordable housing to God's people in need. We toiled in 110-degree heat and drank, with gusto, 110-degree Cokes.

If any of my co-laborers knew my little secret—I, too, was an insurance guy—they didn't let on. When my poorly executed hammer swing sent a nail flying or when I put too much water into our stucco mix, they graciously handed me another nail, or threw a little more sand through the homemade sifter and transferred it to the mix.

Near the end of our week-long venture, I expressed to another volunteer the frustration I felt being a suit—an insurance guy. I envied a young woman on our team who was set to launch her career in non-profit work. The fellow reminded me that, while charitable causes need laborers, they also need donors—people whose professions allow them to earn money they can share.

Over the past twenty years, I've been blessed to make a living in insurance. By the way, I don't sell the stuff; I write about it for those who do. During my career, I've encountered thousands of insurance folks who are proud of their profession and the work they do for individuals and businesses, particularly in their time of greatest need—when a hurricane strikes, when a wage-earner dies, or when a family member faces a critical illness that causes them to ask, "Why?" Folks I've met prove that insurance is, as Campolo wrote in his book, "a noble profession."

I've been even more blessed to be able to support a number of ministries that grew out of the Clarence Jordan and Martin England's combined vision. In addition to financial support, my wife and I spent one of two honeymoon weeks on a Habitat for Humanity project in North Carolina; I spearheaded a work camp in one of the most crime-ridden cities in North America; my daughter spent a week of her high-school spring vacation building in Tennessee; I led a local affiliate serving families in suburban New Jersey and helped form another in northern New England.

My crowning moment, perhaps, was meeting my teen-aged son Christian in Key West at the end of his three-week-long bicycle trip with The Fuller Center for Housing. As part of the ride, which started for him in Williamsburg, Virginia, he raised money—some on his own from friends and family, and some from my friends, fellow insurance people who, as one said, "love to give money to worthy causes."

When Jordan and England staked their spot in the red clay of southern Georgia, they did so because they believed the world could be a better place. When England pursued Martin Luther King, he did so out of concern for his family's future. I suspect neither foresaw the reach their faith and principles would have.

The teen-aged son of an insurance guy is just one very small part of the story. In late September, others who have been touched by the vision gathered near the farm to take part in the Clarence Jordan Symposium, which kicked off a month-long Koinonia Farm 2012 Celebration. Speakers influenced by the Koinonia experiment and its founders addressed everything from agriculture and environmental theology to peace making, partnership housing and much more.

Gathered were non-profit workers, retirees, pastors, academics, stay-at-home moms, and folks from the business arena—maybe even an insurance guy or gal—who were learning together how to extend the reach of Koinonia's philosophies. Their time together followed the principles captured in the words of the Apostle Paul's letter to the Galatians, "There is neither Jew nor Greek, there is neither slave nor free man, there is neither male nor female" (and from the Abridged Dave Version, "there is neither insurance guy nor non-insurance guy"); for you are all one in Christ Jesus."

12

Reflections on the Americus Movement

Sam Mahone

Until the passage of the Civil Rights Act of 1964, segregation by race was the law of the land throughout the Southern United States. Under a system of Southern apartheid, blacks could not eat in restaurants, stay in hotels, swim in public beaches or pools, or attend the same schools, colleges or churches if any of these facilities or institutions were used by whites. It was the written and unwritten law of the land, and black folk intuitively knew what lines not to cross simply because of the South's history of institutionalized racial separation and the brutal and murderous enforcement of it. Indeed, state and local police as well as the courts were all required to uphold and enforce these unjust laws. Education and job opportunities were restricted on the basis of race that can only be described as affirmative action that assured upward mobility for whites and subjugation and dependency for blacks.

In Americus, as it was across the South, white family hierarchy ruled with an iron fist and nepotism reigned throughout city and county government. Fred Chappell was the county sheriff known for his inhumanity and brutality toward blacks, and it was Dr. Martin Luther King, Jr. who called Chappell the "meanest man in the world" after spending the weekend in his jail in December of 1961. Several members of Chappell's family occupied local offices. Frank Chappell was postmaster, Rufus Chappell was a county commissioner, Carl Chappell was a state patrolman, Elizabeth Chappell was the court clerk in charge of voter registration, her husband was a local state patrolman, Allen Chappell was a state public service commissioner, and Boots Chappell was the county home demonstration agent. To be black and living in Americus during this era meant that every aspect of your day to day existence was determined by someone within the Chappell stronghold, and indeed, blacks had no rights that any whites were bound to respect.

In the midst of these oppressive conditions, blacks turned to their houses of worship as sources of strength and fortification, and in early 1960, under the leadership of several local black pastors and businessmen, they formed the Sumter County Voters League. Their mission was to begin an aggressive campaign to seek political power by registering African Americans to vote in spite of poll taxes, so-called literacy tests, physical violence, and intimidation at the registrar's office.

To put this bit of history into a better perspective we should look more closely at how these realities set in motion an irreversible path to self-determination and empowerment for a besieged and beleaguered African American community. In 1960, two years before the Americus Movement began, Americus city officials and white business leaders were increasingly concerned about the impact of the Supreme Court's decision that involuntary segregation in public schools was illegal. Georgia Governor Ernest Vandiver created an all-white fact-finding commission to visit cities throughout the state in an effort to determine "the will of the people." The first public hearing of this group was held in Americus on March 3, 1960. Of the twenty-four South Georgia counties involved, Sumter County was officially represented by the superintendent of Americus schools, bankers and civic leaders, the chairman of the county commissioners, and a representative of the 800 white employees of the Manhattan Shirt Factory. The result of this meeting of more than fifty persons was a resounding message of segregation now, segregation forever, and by any means necessary. Whatever the costs in money, literacy, friendship or lives, the commission was determined to fight to uphold segregation with all the resources at its disposal.

Meanwhile, as a young student movement emerged in Americus in 1961, all eyes in our community were keenly focused on Albany, Georgia, where Martin Luther King, Jr. was leading protests against segregated places of public accommodation, and the Student Non-Violent Coordinating Committee (SNCC) was engaged in an extensive voter registration campaign. When the Albany protests subsided, civil rights activism moved swiftly to Americus. At the time, Sumter County had a population of 25,000, with 13,000 residing in Americus; African Americans accounted for over 52 percent of the population. Of those numbers, there were only 300 black registered voters. The median income for blacks was $1,200, compared to $5,100 for whites. And so in early 1962, Charles Sherrod, who headed SNCC's Southwest Georgia Project, dispatched three field workers to Americus to assist in organizing a broader and more comprehensive voter registration and education initiative. Together with the energized Voters League, they began holding mass meetings that produced a well coordinated and disciplined student activist group, and thus the Americus-Sumter County Movement was formed. The organization immediately began canvassing throughout the county to register voters who could eventually run for office and elect candidates of their choice. They also expanded the mission to tackle the issue of segregation in public places and discrimination in hiring practices.

The first attempt to integrate public facilities in Americus occurred in July of 1963, when eleven young blacks attempted to purchase tickets at the "white" window of the local theater, thus openly defying a lifetime of racist and humiliating customs. They were ordered to disperse by the police and when they refused, they were arrested and thrown in jail. What followed this singular act of bravery by these young students was a tidal wave of daily protests between 1963 and 1965 against police brutality and black voter suppression, and as the Americus city and county jails overflowed, hundreds of protestors, some as young as eleven years old, were outsourced to jails in surrounding Lee and Terrell counties. Three months of intensive protests and arrests left Americus a legacy of bitterness and resentment, but it also provided the Americus Movement the opportunity to impact the overall Southern civil rights movement with two important legal challenges.

The first one involved four college-age students, John Perdew, Don Harris, Ralph Allen and Zev Aelony, who became known as "The Americus Four." On August 8, 1963 they were charged with the century-old Sedition Law (Insurrection), inciting to riot—which carried the death penalty—and were jailed for more than three months. C. B. King, Donald Hollowell, Thomas Jackson, and Constance Baker Motley, associate counsel to the

NAACP Legal Defense Fund, defended the students and in November 1963, a three judge panel ruled the charges unconstitutional.

The second big legal challenge came as a result of the Americus Movement intensifying its voter registration efforts throughout the county. The city's response to these efforts was a virulent and violent backlash against potential black voters, who, along with civil rights workers and ministers, were brutally attacked daily by city and county law enforcement as they waited in line at the court house.

Determined not to be denied, nor intimidated, the Americus Movement leadership decided to run its own candidate for public office, and on July 21, 1965, Mary Kate Fishe-Bell became the first black woman to run for public office in the history of Sumter County, in the Democratic primary. However, on the day of the election, she was arrested along with three other women, including the wife of the Americus Movement President, Mrs. Mamie Campbell. Their crime was attempting to vote in the white only voting line. Their arrests triggered daily massive demonstrations at the court house demanding their release, prompting the all-white merchants association to offer to bond them out of jail, which they refused and demanded that their release be immediate and unconditional. Three days later the four women filed suit in federal court to enjoin local officials from further prosecution and to end segregated elections in Sumter County. Two weeks later, a federal judge ordered their release, and an end to segregated elections.

The impact of these landmark legal cases had profound implications that reached far beyond Americus. After the decision that freed the Americus Four, it was clear to civil rights workers and legal scholars throughout the South and the nation that if the state had prevailed on these charges, it would have stifled and possibly ended protest movements across the South. The intent by the state of Georgia in lodging these charges was to once and for all crush the movement by indiscriminately arresting anyone deemed leaders and jailing them under the threat of the death sentence. These legal victories were of profound importance to the civil rights movement.

The Americus Movement collectively with the Selma, Alabama protests brought national attention to the voting rights struggle and lawless resistance to the right of African Americans to vote. By the end of 1965, more than 3,500 newly registered African American voters were added to the Sumter County voter rolls. The Americus Movement ignited demonstrations in at least seventy other counties across the south where SNCC and

Martin Luther King, Jr.'s Southern Christian Leadership Council's Summer Community Organization and Political Education project (SCOPE) were operating. The daily protests and arrests in Americus that followed the Voting Rights Act out of congress helped to break the resistance of the Southern filibuster and thereby secured the implementation of both the Civil Rights Act of 1964 and the Voting Rights Act of 1965.

The supportive relationship and shared experiences between the Koinonia community and the Americus Movement cannot be overstated. I was seventeen when I joined the movement and even though born here, I knew very little about Koinonia. I was introduced by rights workers who had been welcomed to visit and stay at the farm by the Jordans, Wittkampers, Browns, Scottie McNeil, and Collins McGee. Koinonia became a safe house and a place of refuge where protestors would retreat after being battered and bruised following jail time. They were welcomed by a caring community that provided meals, shelter, and clothing for those who required them. We were inspired by Greg Wittkamper, a student at the Americus High School and resident of Koinonia, whose nonviolent response to bullying became a quiet model for blacks attending Americus High.

It is indeed quite fitting that those of you who are gathered here to celebrate the life of Clarence Jordan all share his passion for life and liberty, and the abhorrence for racism, materialism, and militarism. Dr. Jordan was the embodiment of all these things and the life he led and the living history of Koinonia should be required study for young people, not only here but around the globe.

Clarence Jordan never stopped pushing the envelope, always thinking how to uplift his fellow men and women. His legacy of inspiration for Habitat for Humanity International became the first global initiative to address the fundamental human right to decent housing for everyone.

His legacy is still relevant in the civil rights issues of our day. This country is on an unsustainable course with catastrophic consequences. With corporate profits the highest in history, the rich have doubled their fortunes; long-term unemployment has devastated many communities, particularly in African American communities where unemployment is averaging between 20 and 27 percent. There is a new Jim Crow in existence in the form of a privatized prison industry. Over a decade ago the prison lobby paid politicians to declare a so-called war on drugs that resulted in a prison for profit economy that disproportionately locked up black and brown people, mostly young men. They took drug infested and diseased individuals, locked them up with long sentences, educated them in criminal behavior, and then released them back into our communities, without any marketable skills. This has become a perfect storm for repeated recidivism and a culture of incarceration. There are now more young black men in prison today than were enslaved a decade before the Civil War. This is a crime against humanity; worse still, it is twenty-first century slavery.

We see voter suppression continuing today. Currently thirty-four states have introduced legislation to restrict voting and twenty-three states have passed legislation to restrict voting. We need to continue fighting to support funding for public schools against the current political attempts to eliminate them in favor of charter or private schools. The journey Clarence started in southwest Georgia is a long one and it is far from over. The Koinonia story is one that can guide our feet while we run this race.

13

Baptized in the Spit

Greg Wittkamper

One part of the Koinonia story that hasn't drawn much attention is the plight of the children who grew up there during the 1950s and 1960s. I'm one of those kids, and there were times it could be tough. In a community famous for being persecuted, sometimes we children caught the worst of it.

In a sense, the Wittkampers were a refugee family. My father, Will, was a Disciples of Christ minister whose congregations kept ousting him because of his stubborn beliefs in pacifism and the brotherhood of all races. He heard about Koinonia and visited the farm, finding kindred spirits in Clarence Jordan, Conrad Browne, and the others. My mother, Margaret, a Methodist missionary, wasn't necessarily keen to move to Georgia, but she agreed to go as long as Dad promised to plant lots of strawberries for her.

I was almost six when we arrived in the summer of 1953. I loved everything about Koinonia: the land, the chores, the livestock, the tractors. There was an abundance of children—more than half of the community's forty or so residents—and we reveled in picnics and hayrides and arrowhead-hunting. Most of us attended an elementary school on the road to Americus, where we clashed from time to time with other students whose parents thought we were communists or race-mixers. Sometimes we were called names or goaded into fights, but it wasn't a constant struggle. At least for awhile.

Almost everyone reading this volume knows what happened next. When Clarence was willing to vouch for two black students attempting to enter the university system of Georgia, Koinonia became the target of vandalism, bombings, and drive-by shootings. I was entering the fourth grade when the terror campaign began in 1956, and I vividly remember the sound of rifle shots ripping through the peach trees as a group of us were playing volleyball one evening.

As the violence subsided and the economic boycott against Koinonia hardened, the conflict seemed to move into the schools. By 1960, three of the community's children, Lora Browne, Jan Jordan, and my older brother, Billy Wittkamper, were ready for high school. They wanted to attend Americus High, but the city's school board refused to admit them on the grounds that their presence would disrupt classes. Our parents sued in federal court and won the case. It was a necessary victory, but it came at a cost. The other students treated Lora, Jan, and Billy far worse than they had ever been treated in grade school. My brother left after a year and finished high school in Illinois. Lora left after her junior year when the Brownes moved to Tennessee, where her father became head of the Highlander Center. Only Jan remained at Americus High through the end of her senior year, enduring endless harassment right up until her graduation day.

That left me. By the fall of 1964, I was the only Koinonia kid at Americus High. It was a dangerous time to stand alone. A decade after the Supreme Court had outlawed segregation in public schools, Americus High was finally being forced to admit a handful of black students, and racial resentment hung over the campus like a toxic vapor.

Like several young people from Koinonia, I had been active in the civil rights movement that had been embroiling Americus. I knew the black students who were desegregating the high school and wanted to show my support for them, so I arranged to ride to school with three of them on the first day of class. We arrived in a funeral home limousine and were met by a mob throwing rocks and bottles and every kind of invective. From the day I stepped out of that limousine— the only white boy among the unwelcome black students—the abuse I had always endured at school escalated. I was marked as a traitor to my race.

In the first weeks of class, I was tripped, spit on, snapped with rubber bands, and shoved on the stairs. The only students who would talk to me called me vile names. The others turned their backs when I walked down the hall and shunned me. One boy went so far as to slug me in the cheek. When I reported the assault to the principal, he acted like it was all my fault for being there.

The worst time was lunch. When I sat down in the cafeteria with my tray, students moved away from my table and often the next table as well. I always ate alone. I was completely isolated.

One day in the lunchroom, I was surprised when one of my classmates motioned for me. "Hey, Greg," he said, "come over here and let's talk."

I should have been wary, but I was hungry for any sort of interaction. Maybe he wanted to ask me about our religious beliefs—I was willing to explain them—so I picked up my tray and started to go over. As I was sitting down, I noticed something flying toward me; someone had thrown a sloppy joe sandwich. I jerked my head back and evaded the missile. It struck another student, who was so angry he smashed *his* sloppy joe into my face, the reddish orange glop making a mess of my white shirt. The lunchroom emptied as quickly as if a fire alarm had sounded.

The principal suggested I go home for the day, but I refused. I wanted everyone in my afternoon classes to see what had happened, what had been happening all along. I wanted to wear my food-stained shirt as a witness.

That afternoon, when I got off the school bus at Koinonia, Clarence spotted my splattered clothes and walked briskly toward me with a look of concern. He must have thought it was blood on my shirt. When he came closer and saw that it wasn't, he opened his arms and hugged me. He knew what I was going through.

A few days later, Clarence approached me in the community dining hall and said that he had been discussing my predicament with a friend. "He had a situation like this in high school," Clarence said, "and the kid who was getting picked on finally fought back. They left him alone after that. Now I'm not telling you what to do. But I've seen you throwing bales of hay out here, and I know you're as strong as an ox. So maybe the next time one of them picks on you—not some puny guy, but someone your own size—maybe you should just haul off and beat the tar out him."

I was astonished. Clarence Jordan, an apostle of nonviolence, who didn't even approve of Koinonia children having toy guns, was giving me permission to whip up on the people who were whipping up on me.

I thought about it for a week and sought Clarence out. "If I'm going to fight them," I told him, "I have to win. They're not going to roll over just because I'm stronger. They have to save face. So if I fight back, I have to be willing to hurt them badly. I *do* want to hurt them, but I don't want to hurt them that badly."

As I saw it, I had no choice but to take it. And I had to take a lot more. Things only got worse for the least popular member of the senior class.

I couldn't wait to get out of Georgia after I graduated from Americus High. I left for college and settled a few years later in West Virginia, where several of us from Koinonia found peace and fulfillment in the beautiful Allegheny Mountains. From time to time, I would think back to high school and the traumas I suffered, and my throat would tighten and my eyes would moisten. My wife, Ann, a wise Virginian who knows the value of therapy, encouraged me to open up and talk about it.

One day, some forty years after I left Koinonia, I stopped in the tiny town near our home to check my post office box. There was a letter postmarked from Georgia. I recognized the name on the return address: David Morgan, one of my high school classmates.

"I expect you will be quite surprised to hear from me. If you remember me at all, it will likely be for unpleasant reasons," he wrote. "Throughout the last 40 years, I have occasionally thought of you and those dark days you endured at our hands. As I matured, I became more and more ashamed, and wished that I had taken a different stand back then."

I stared at the letter for a long time and began to tear up. I didn't know it then, but more letters were on the way.

14

In Scorn of the Consequences

Dallas Lee

Introduction

Today, I will give you as much of Clarence Jordan's actual thinking as possible, relying on his words from *The Substance of Faith*. This is the book I did *not* write. I just typed it up. That is, I transcribed presentations preserved informally (and rather haphazardly) on tape recorders, many of them at American Baptist pastors conferences. I edited only for clarity, which is to say I inserted periods so that strung-out thoughts could continue in new sentences. *The Substance of Faith* is *all* Clarence—his intellect, his courage, his humor, his imaginative, authentic self. (Buy a copy and read it. Koinonia Farm holds the copyright and employs the proceeds in good service.)

Those old tape recordings were priceless. Clarence was an expository teacher who left no scripts behind. He'd study, make a few notes along the way, and take to the podium with his head, heart, and Greek New Testament. He was an extraordinary extemporaneous speaker—a storyteller, witty and provocative. Try imagining John the Baptist with a sense of humor. Clarence clobbered you with ideas, and you laughed receiving the blows.

Baptist, but Uniquely So

Clarence Jordan was a Southern Baptist, but...

- He did *not* preach the deity of Jesus—in fact, he hardly if ever mentioned it. He preached the humanity of God.
- He did *not* preach salvation in the hereafter; he preached the kingdom of God on Earth.
- He did *not* teach the resurrection of Jesus as a promise of immortality. He taught that the resurrection is Jesus' promise to be with his followers always, wherever *their light* overcomes the *darkness in this world.*
- He taught that the early apostles *were* the resurrected body of Jesus. "Never did Paul or Peter or Stephen point to an empty tomb as evidence of the resurrection of Jesus," he said. "The evidence was the spirit-filled fellowship."
- He didn't preach the sorrow of repentance; he preached the joy of new life, of "metamorphosis" into a whole new way of being.
- He taught that "born again" is an off-the-mark phrase. The Gospel words in Greek, he said, refer *not* to the mother's role in birth but to *the father's role in siring.*
- And he taught that the church's job is to be the handmaiden of the Lord—that is, "the womb of God," giving birth to God's children, just as Mary gave birth to Jesus.

For Clarence, the Incarnation—God become man—was the foundation. Over time, he grew as angry as an Old Testament prophet at a religious culture he saw as obsessed with the deity of Jesus at the expense of the humanity of God. As a result, he said, too many churches busy themselves with heavenly matters, hoard their earthly wealth and remain blind to human suffering.

The Homeland as a Mission Field

All this being said, it is important to understand that Clarence Jordan was *not* a born revolutionary. To the contrary, in 1942 he was a young Baptist pastor who felt called to the mission field. He had studied agriculture in college and earned degrees at Southern Baptist Theological Seminary. He was on a well-trod path, equipping himself to preach and teach the gospel as well as to make practical contributions to the lives of people. The only radical note (to some) was his conscientious objection to war.

What first distinguished Clarence, I believe, was how he identified his own homeland as a mission field. Coming out of the Great Depression, the rural farm regions of the South were desolate. The farm economy was wrecked. Jobs, classrooms, and schoolbooks were scarce, especially for the poor who had lost meager livelihoods in the collapse of tenant-farming. And, as those of us old enough know, racism was embedded in every institution, from kitchen table to classroom, from courthouse square to church sanctuary.

Demonstration Plot

In the face of all this, Clarence had a radical idea. I would say original idea, except that Clarence duly credited the Acts of the Apostles. He wanted to establish a *"demonstration plot"* in the heart of the South, a place where followers of Christ would live as the apostles did after Pentecost; pool their possessions and money, take care of each other, share their bounty of education, expertise and resources, and manifest in their daily lives what it means to "love thy neighbor as thyself."

Koinonia Farm was, if not by-the-book, a well-organized missionary enterprise. It had financial backing in the business community of Louisville, Kentucky, where Clarence had pioneered inner-city ministries while in seminary. Clarence had an experienced mentor and partner—the American Baptist missionary Martin England, who with his wife had been forced home on leave by the outbreak of war in Europe and Asia. They, and the folks who engaged with them at Koinonia Farm, were not rabble-rousers, not demonstrators marching in the streets. Never was there the intent to confront, or to try forcing the integration of schools, businesses or churches.

The Koinonians were good neighbors, first and foremost. They regularly loaned their tractors, harvesters and other equipment. They experimented to develop and introduce hog-farrowing barns and poultry farming in southwest Georgia. Clarence himself developed an early-model peanut picking contraption. And my personal favorite: Koinonia established a milk library. A poor family could check out a milk cow, return her when she was dry and check out another.

Barnyard Stuff Hits the Fan

The Koinonians also rode the back roads to pick up black children and get them to the consolidated county schools. No buses were provided for them. And, of course, they welcomed all who worked on the farm to share meals and, eventually, housing. In other words, they integrated through a process that might otherwise be called hospitality and good manners. The result, as you know, was that all hell broke loose. Random gunfire in the nights (they could count bullet holes in the wall). Ku Klux Klan caravans along the road. An economic boycott. The faithful of Koinonia Farm lived for a decade in an atmosphere of threats and intimidation, experiencing acts of emotional and physical violence. This was years before MLK and the heyday of the civil rights movement. Years before the intense television coverage that eventually awakened the hearts and opened the eyes of good people, and led to changes in laws and culture.

(Even as recently as 1970, I often trembled with anxiety going around Americus and Sumter County, conducting interviews with business and community leaders, and the sheriff. Even then, you could still run into angry faces on the sidewalk, and threatening gestures from suspicious cars on the Dawson Highway.)

It is through these experiences that Clarence arrived at his own definition of faith. Faith, he said, is "life lived in scorn of the consequences." That's not a definition one studies or meditates or prays his way to. It is a definition that comes alive in the crucible.

Ongoing Influence

With this background, it's interesting to contemplate Clarence Jordan's influence in the world. If we consider Habitat for Humanity, we can say his ongoing influence is a worldwide ministry—perhaps the most effective, spirit-filled, hands-on, sustainable volunteer concept in history. But, if we focus on the way of life Clarence chose, well, then, most of us would need only our fingers to count people we know of such radical commitment. (Jubilee Partners in Comer, Georgia, with its refugee settlement program, is a strong example. Don Mosley's book on the experience of that community, *Faith Beyond Borders*, was published in 2010.)

Let me hasten to clarify that Habitat for Humanity *is* Clarence Jordan's legacy—as much his as it is Millard Fuller's. Millard could turn burlap and cake flour to gold, but it was Clarence's intellect, imagination, rigorous scholarship and charisma that put Millard on the path to ministry. And by 1968, with the Koinonia Community down to two families, Clarence was dispirited and at a loss for purpose. The experiment in "koinonia" seemed no longer a viable or strong enough witness. It was Millard—Millard's stubborn practicality and genius for making things happen—that awakened Clarence to new possibilities and energized him. Each of those men, I can testify, had the courage of lions. Together, it seems, they could change water into wine.[1]

Let me continue from here with a sampling of Clarence's actual words, from The Substance of Faith:

> The Womb of God [excerpts, pages 18–21]
>
> *From Luke, God's messenger Gabriel announces to Mary she will become pregnant*
>
> Here we have God taking the initiative, coming to earth, impregnating a woman and siring a son. That's the narrative. Now we say, how can that be? And we get all scientific about it. How can that happen? I don't know. We're not involved here with scientific fact. We're involved with religious truth. . .
>
> I'm not worried about whether this is scientific fact or not. I'm inclined to believe that Joseph was in the flesh the father of Jesus. I don't think Jesus ever doubted that. But God was his Father in a very real sense. And what the virgin birth is trying to say to us is not that a man became divine, but that God Almighty took the initiative and established permanent residence on this earth.
>
> Now we, today, have reversed . . . the incarnation. Instead of the Word becoming flesh and dwelling among us, we turn it

---

1. When Clarence and Millard decided to sit down and talk seriously about what they might do together, they did it in the pastor's study at Oakhurst Baptist Church in Decatur, Ga.—one of the handful of Baptist churches in the South where Clarence felt at home. John Nichol was pastor in the 1960s and '70s, and was leading that congregation through troubled—and often joyous times—in a racially and economically changing community. It was the sort of challenge that caused many churches to sell and move to the suburbs of America's cities. A lay leader, Walker Knight, wrote an excellent, candid book of the Oakhurst journey, *Struggle for Integrity* (Word Press), and he is still writing and participating in the life of Oakhurst Church today.

Writer's note: I should point out that I was *not* one of the brave souls who hewed to Clarence's way. As Millard Fuller told my friend and fellow reporter Keith Graham in an interview several years after *The Cotton Patch Evidence* was published, "Dallas couldn't take the heat, so he got out of the kitchen." True. That did not hurt my feelings. Millard was a courageous, candid man and a generous friend to whom I owe a great deal.

around and we take a bit of flesh and deify it. We have deified Jesus and, thus, effectively rid ourselves of him even more than if we had crucified him ... If God Almighty would just stay God and quit becoming man, then we could handle him. We can build our cathedrals to him. This is the bind we get in today. We reverse the action—from heaven to earth—and we turn it around and build it from earth to heaven. And salvation becomes something that we will attain some day, rather than God coming to earth to be among us ...

In the Book of Acts, we see this drama reenacted. They [the apostles] all are quietly together, the handmaiden of the Lord ... praying, saying, *"Be it unto me according to your will"* ... [We] want to be the womb of God ... the agency through which He comes into this world and does His work in the affairs of men. We're ready, Lord, to be impregnated ... And this is exactly what begins to happen. This is the job of the Church. To become the womb of God through which He can bring His child [the sons and daughters of God] into the world.

Metamorphosis [excerpts, pages 94–97]

In another presentation, Clarence picks back up on the apostles setting the precedent for the church as the womb of God—this time using Jesus' confrontation with Nicodemus [italics from CJ translation of Gospel of John, chapter 3]

Jesus came preaching and all his preaching revolved around one mighty phrase. You remember when he had gone through the temptation experience, it says, *'And Jesus came into Galilee preaching, Change your whole way of thinking for the new order of the spirit is impinging upon you.'* All this preaching was to get men to go through the process of what we call repentance, which is an awful translation of the Greek word *metanoia*.

We have an English word, metamorphosis, which comes from that Greek word *meta*, meaning *to change*, and *morphe*, meaning *form*... A little caterpillar will crawl along in the dirt and the leaves and finally the great forces of nature—the warm weather, flowers and all—begin to work changes and he climbs up on a stem and gets real still and then something great begins to happen. He begins to split open his skin and out of that little caterpillar emerges a fragile, beautiful monarch butterfly ... equipped to move in the spring breezes, to go to the flowers ... The new order of spring has demanded that the caterpillar change his form in order to be ready for the demands and the needs that are impinging upon him.

Now this Greek word *metanoia* is almost exactly the same word . . . It means to "go through"—not the transformation of the body, but the transformation of the mind and of the soul that equips you for a new order. It doesn't mean *re-pent*. To me, repent means to get all sorry for getting caught at something. This is not what *metanoia* means. It doesn't have one tiny little bit of sorrow in it . . . Would you say to the caterpillar, "Well, little caterpillar, you know I sure do feel sorry for you—you're fixing to become a butterfly." . . . No! His birthday is here! He's about to enter into a new order that God Almighty has prepared for him. The happiest thing a little caterpillar can do is to metamorphose! And the happiest thing that can happen to a person is for the light of God to shine on him . . . to be taken out of his darkness and put in a new order of things . . .

Jesus did not say, "Nicodemus, you've got to be born again." He said, "You've got to be sired from above." The word he used here is the Greek verb *gennao*, which means "to set in motion the life processes." Once in a great while this verb will be used to refer to a woman giving birth. But the Greek word for "to give birth" is *tikto*, and this is the word the Bible uses when it says Mary gave birth to Jesus. But this word *gennao* refers not to the act of the woman, but to the act of the father . . . *It refers not to the point of birth but to the point of conception.* This is very important. He's talking not about a birth, but a siring.

"Jesus said to him (Nicodemus) except one be sired out of both water and out of spirit, he can't enter the God Movement. That which is sired out of flesh, that is flesh. That which is sired out of spirit, that is spirit." The water is fluid. This refers not to the fluid of birth, but the fluid of conception—semen. It's a fluid in which life is resident . . .

[Jesus] goes on to say in verse 16: *"For God so loved the world* (that is, God loved the world just as a husband loves a wife) *that he gave his only begotten*—(This verb in the Greek can be either active or passive. You can translate it *only begotten* or *only begetting* and be correct either way.)—*so that whoever believes on him, or receives him* (like an unfertilized egg receives sperm) *might not perish away* (like an infertile egg perishes) *but that it might have spiritual life."*

The egg without God perishes. God without man in a sense perishes in that he is unfulfilled. Man is as necessary to God as God is to man, just as the egg is as necessary to the sperm as the sperm is to the egg. Either one, apart from the other, is unfulfilled. But when you get them together you've got spiritual life. Then you've got this *metanoia*—this newness of life.

Resurrection [excerpts from pages 100–101]

Now, this raising of Jesus Christ from the dead was not to guarantee our immortality. It was to guarantee our spirituality, our re-fathering into a new life—newness of life, Paul called it. And this raising of Jesus Christ from the dead was but the Father's final vindication of the kind of life that Jesus lived, the kind of spirit that he had, and the Father saying, *"This spirit will live on this earth"* . . . If God Almighty can break the bonds of death in all of its aspects for his son Jesus Christ, then surely he can break the bonds of death that shackle us and make us slaves to sin and selfishness and greed in this old world, and re-sire us that we may be born as sons of God. . . .

[Clarence, reading from the epistle 1 Peter:]

"We've *been re-sired into a life of hope, based on the raising of Jesus Christ from the dead."* We think of that as referring to the Second Coming and the Final Judgment. No, this isn't what he's saying at all. The final showdown is whenever Christians confront the forces and powers of *this* world. The end of the world is the beginning of light . . . It's when light and darkness are conflicting—that's the final age, that's the showdown. When the Christians were talking about Jesus coming and ushering in the end of the world, they weren't talking about the cataclysmic windup of this physical world. They were talking about the coming of the light, *a dawn that's coming in the hearts of men.*

I have seen this wherever brotherhood is preached. One of the reasons I think that [they] had it in so hot for us at Koinonia Farm was because they saw, in the kind of life we were proclaiming, the end of their world. Wherever brotherhood comes in, that's the end of the world for exploitation and arrogance. This final showdown is any showdown between the forces of Jesus Christ and the forces of evil.

Afterword

"*Feed the hungry.*" It seemed clear this was what we were called to do as we set out to return to the original vision for Koinonia Farm. Feed the hungry physically by learning to naturally grow and distribute healthy food. Feed the hungry spiritually by continuing to offer hospitality, by conducting an internship several times a year, giving talks, teaching classes, keeping Clarence Jordan's books in print, maybe even by organizing a symposium.

We at Koinonia Farm believe the Clarence Jordan Symposium is one of the fruits born from the return to the communal roots.

For us, farming is both a root and a fruit of our life together. Wayne Weiseman delivers in "Koinonia Farm and the Permaculture Movement" a clear description of the agriculture practices we are following today. Permaculture is devoted to "care for earth, care for people, and sharing the surplus." It is a new fruit of the farm, but agriculture is one of our roots.

However, our deepest roots can be found in the Gospels, in particular the Sermon on the Mount, and from Acts of the Apostles:

> All the believers were together. They held all things in common. They were selling their property and possessions, and were distributing them to everyone according to each one's need. Every day they continued together in the temple. They broke bread in their houses. They shared food with gladness and in simplicity of heart. They praised God and had favor among all the people.

From 1942 to 1993, through many ups and downs, the community remained faithful to the vision of the early church and survived. Then there began a sojourn from that founding impetus that brought Koinonia nearer to extinction than any bombs, bullets or boycotts of its early years. This detour ended in 2005 when a small band of people committed to return together to the communal structure.

Where to start in rebuilding a community? Beginning in 1942, Koinonia's mission was to live a way of life rooted in the Gospel and, inevitably, out of this shared life would come service to others. What we found at the heart of that beginning was the effort to simply be a good neighbor. The Jordans and Englands and those who came after them took "love your neighbor as yourself" as a command that required intention and action.

This notion of being firmly rooted in the Scripture and being in relationship with and loving our neighbor sounded like a good place to start for us as well. Those early Koinonians farmed, provided hospitality and offered an internship or discipleship school experience. They introduced new and effective ways of growing food. They welcomed whoever showed up regardless of race, faith, no faith, education or socio-economic background and shared food, shelter and fellowship with them. The internship was a period of immersion in this experiment in Christian living, an experience in living this very intentional way of life. These three activities are at the core of our life today.

But as we began this restart of the communal way of life at Koinonia, we also soon became aware of something else. As we looked at the roots and learned the history, we realized we had a responsibility that Clarence and Florence Jordan and Martin and Mabel England did not have when they founded the community. We had the responsibility to tell their story and the story of all those who came before us. And what a story it is. And what fruit it bore. We also had the opportunity to share with folks about all the good works that had come forth from or been inspired by Clarence and Koinonia.

Even more, though, we celebrated the obligation to disseminate Clarence Jordan's words, wisdom and wit. They are some of the best spiritual food we know. He continues to inspire and encourage us as we journey in God's kingdom and we cherish this chance to expose others to that same inspiration and encouragement that you have found in *Roots in the Cotton Patch* and *Fruits of the Cotton Patch*.

Much of what you have read in these two volumes is about our history, but the roots continue to grow deeper and there is much new fruit. One of the many life-giving experiences for us today is what you read in Jonathan Wilson-Hartgrove's chapter entitled "The Kingdom is like Kudzu: Koinonia Farm and a New Monasticism in America." We hope our call to live a simpler, gentler way of life serves as a demonstration plot for a way of life that is truly possible. As Jonathan stated, "If Clarence Jordan taught us anything, he taught that our task is to translate God's news into our own time and place. We do this, like Jesus, by enfleshing the message—turning words into deeds by the work of our hands and the grace of God, one day at

Afterword

a time, in scorn of the consequences. The essential thing is the demonstration plot. People need to see what God's movement looks like in practice. It is indeed, the gospel in blue jeans."

In our living, we still tear down walls as Shane Claiborne shares in his chapter. We do not choose to tear down those walls with aggressive rhetoric, with bombs, bullets and boycott of others, but rather we respond to the needs and challenges of the time with thoughtful action rooted in prayer. Or so we hope.

Today our life continues to generate stories and to bear fruit, but we are committed to honoring our past, honoring those who came before us. This collection of writings from the keynote addresses and seminars of the 2012 Clarence Jordan Symposium is one of the efforts to meet the responsibility to share the story and spread the wisdom. We pray that they have fed you spiritually.

To contact Koinonia Farm write us at 1324 GA Hwy 49 S, Americus, GA 31719, visit our Web site at koinoniafarm.org or call us at (229) 924-0391. Y'all come!

Bren Dubay
Koinonia Farm
2013

Celebrating the Life and Ministry of Clarence Jordan

A Working Bibliography

G. W. Carlson

The following bibliography is designed to allow the user an opportunity to develop a broader context for understanding the life and ministry of Clarence Jordan and the Koinonia Farm experiment. It is condensed from a larger bibliographical work that is more inclusive and provides materials on contemporary use of the Clarence Jordan story in today's church.

Besides the archives at Koinonia there are two important collections of materials on Clarence Jordan and Koinonia at the Hargrett Rare Book and Manuscript Library, University of Georgia in Athens, Georgia and Southern Baptist Archives in Nashville, Tennessee. The libraries at Southern Baptist Theological Seminary and Bethel Seminary have substantial collections of Clarence Jordan materials. Especially of interest is the collection of Clarence Jordan speeches and interviews.

Biographical and Historical Study of Clarence Jordan, Millard Fuller and Koinonia Farm

"According to Clarence." *Newsweek*, February 26, 1968, 61.

Armstrong, O. K., and Marjorie Armstrong. "Clarence Jordan and Koinonia," in *The Baptists in America*, 377–79. New York: Doubleday, 1979.

Barnette, Henlee H. *Clarence Jordan: Turning Dreams into Deeds* Macon, GA: Smyth and Helwys, 1992.

———. "Southern Baptist Seminary and the Civil Rights Movement: From 1859–1952." *Review and Expositor* 93 (Winter 1996) 77–126.

Blau, Eleanor. "30-Year Old Christian Commune in Georgia Thrives After Adversity." *New York Times*, May 27, 1972.

Boers, Arthur. "The Prophet or the President." *The Other Side* (January/February 1988) 32–36.

Bryan, G. McLeod. "Clarence Jordan, 1912–1969" in *Voices in the Wilderness: Twentieth-century Prophets Speak to the New Millennium*, 53–76. Atlanta, GA: Mercer University Press, 1999.

———. "Theology in Overalls" *Sojourners* 8, no. 12 (December 1979) 10–11.

Campbell, Will D. "Where There's So Much Smoke" *Sojourners* 8, no. 12 (December 1979) 19.

Carter, Jimmy. "Introduction" *Living Faith*, 5–7. New York: Three Rivers, 1996.

———. "Riding Freely" in *Sources of Strength*, 218–221. New York: Times Book, 1997.

Castle, David. *A Brief History of Koinonia: The Post-Jordan Years: 1970-2007*. Americus, GA: Koinonia Partners, Inc, 2007.

Chancey, Andrew S. "A Demonstration Plot for the Kingdom of God: The Establishment and Early Years of Koinonia Farm" *Georgia Historical Quarterly* 75 no. 2 (1991) 321–353.

———. "Clarence Jordan (1912–1969)" *The New Georgia Encyclopedia*, March 11, 2005.

———. "Koinonia Farm" *The New Georgia Encyclopedia*, March 26, 2009.

———. "Koinonia in the '90s" *The Christian Century*, October 14, 1992, 892–894.

———. "Race, Religion, and Agricultural Reform: The Communal Vision of Koinonia Farm" in *Georgia in Black and White: Explorations in the Race Relations of a Southern State, 1865-1950*, edited by John C. Inscoe, 247–249. Athens: University of Georgia Press, 1994.

Claiborne, Shane, et al. "October 29—Clarence Jordan" in *Common Prayer*, 495–497. Grand Rapids: Zondervan, 2010.

Coble, Ann Louise. *Cotton Patch for the Kingdom*. Scottdale, PA: Herald, 2002. Vol. 111, No. 21, July 13, 1994, 681.

———. "Cotton Patch Justice, Cotton Patch Peace: The Sermon on the Mount in the Teachings and Practices of Clarence Jordan." In *Theology and The New Histories*, edited by Gary Macy, 202–211. New York: Orbis, 1998, .

Day, Dorothy. "Fear in Our Time." *The Catholic Worker*, April 1968, 5, 7.

———. "On Pilgrimage—May 1957" *The Catholic Worker*, May 1957, 3, 6.

Downing, Frederick L. "Rewriting the Cultural Myths: Clarence Jordan and the Cotton Patch Gospels." *SBL Forum* 7.5 (2009). Online: http://www.sbl-site.org/publications/article.aspx?ArticleId=827.

Dubay, Bren. "Koinonia: An Intentional Christian Community" *Koinonia Farm Chronicle* 3, no. 1 (Spring 2010) 2.

———. "Koinonia 70 Years Later: 1942–2012" *Koinonia Farm Chronicle* 4, no. 1 (Spring 2011) 1.

———. "Sink into Cynicism or Soar into Hope?" In *Cynicism and Hope*, edited by Meg E. Cox, 65–71, Eugene, OR: Wipf and Stock, 2008.

Gentry, Jerry. "Koinonia Turns Fifty." *Southern Exposure* XX, no. 2 (Summer 1992) 58–63.

Harding, Rosemarie and Rachel Harding. "Radical Hospitality" *Sojourners* 32, no. 4 (July–August 2003) 42–46.

Harding, Rosemarie and Vincent Harding. "Forward the Dawn" *Sojourners* 13, no. 13, (April 1984) 24–25.

Harding, Rosemary Freeney as told to Rachel E. Harding. "There was a Tree in Starksville" *Sojourners* February 2012. Onine: http://sojo.net/magazine/2012/02/there-was-tree-starksville.

Harding, Vincent. *Hope and History* Maryknoll, NY: Orbis, 1990.

———. "In The Company of the Faithful: Journeying Toward the Promised Land" *Sojourners* 14, no. 5 (May 1985) 14–21.

Hawkins, Mel. "A Faithful Remnant: Southern White Supporters of the Civil Rights Movement." *EthicsDaily.com* January 14, 2002. Online: http://www.ethicsdaily.com/a-faithful-remnant-southern-white-supporters-of-the-civil-rights-movement-cms-169.

Hearne, Joshua. "Clarence Jordan, Farmer, Founder of Koinonia Farm, Opponent of the Status Quo." *Telling the Stories that Matter* October 27, 2009. Onine: http://www.ttstm.com/2010/10/october-27-clarence-jordan-farmer.html.

Ho, Esther Mohler. "Koinonia Farm" *Church Advocate*, February 1967, 5–7, 11, 15.

Hollyday, Joyce "A Scandalous Life of Faith" *Sojourners* 8, no. 12 (December 1979).

———. "Clarence Jordan: Theologian in Overalls" in *Cloud of Witnesses* (Edited by Jim Wallis and Joyce Hollyday) Maryknoll, NY: Orbis, 1991, 68–72.

———. "The Dream That Has Endured: Clarence Jordan and Koinonia" *Sojourners* 8, no. 12 (December 1979).

Jordan, Jim. "Growing Up at Koinonia." *Christianity Today*, March 9, 2005.

Kennedy, John W. "Hard Times Down on the Farm." *Christianity Today*, January 9, 1995, 58–59.

K'Meyer, Tracy Elaine. *Interracialism and Christian Community in the Postwar South.* Charlottesville: University Press of Virginia, 1997.

———. "'What Koinonia Was all About': The Role of Memory in a Changing Community." *The Oral History Review* 24, no. 1 (Summer 1997) 1–22.

"Koinonia Farm" *The New Georgia Encyclopedia*. Athens: Georgia Humanities Council and the University of Georgia Press, 2009.

"Koinonians Seek to Follow Way of Life 'Jesus Taught." *Ebony*, July 1957, 51–52.

Lee, Dallas. *The Cotton Patch Evidence: The Story of Clarence Jordan and the Koinonia Farm Experiment.* New York: Harper and Row, 1971.

Lee, Rhonda Mawhood. "'Admit Guilt—and Tell the Truth.' The Louisville Fellowship of Reconciliations Struggle with Pacifism and Racial Justice, 1941–1945." *Journal of Southern History* (May 1, 2010) 15.

Lee, Robert. "The Crisis at Koinonia." *Christian Century* November 7, 1956, 1290–1291.

Lull, Howard W. "Koinonia Updated" *Christian Century*, October 13, 1976, 868–872.

Marsh, Charles. "Charles Marsh Recounts Clarence Jordan's Conversion Experience That Led Him to Struggle Against Segregation in the Jim Crow South." *The Project on Lived Theology* 2010.

———. "In the Fields of the Lord: The God Movement in South Georgia." in *The Beloved Community* New York: Basic Books, 2005, 51–86.

———. "Work of Faith" *Christianity Today* February 23, 2005.

McClendon, Jr., James Wm. "The Theory Tested: Clarence Jordan—Radical in Community," in *Biography as Theology: How Life Stories Can Remake Today's Theology*, 112–139. Nashville, TN: Abingdon, 1974.

McDowell, Edward. "Introduction." In *The Cotton Patch Version of Hebrews and the General Epistles*, by Clarence Jordan. Americus, GA: The Cotton Patch Gospel Koinonia Partners, 1973.

McNeely, Jack. "Making a Difference: Dubay Ready to Lead Koinonia Through Rebirth." *Americus Times-Recorder* Americus, GA, May 7, 2004.

Moore, Amanda. "Faith is the Life Based on Unseen Realities: Celebrating the Spirit of Clarence Jordan" *Koinonia Farm Chronicle* 2, no. 2 (Fall 2009) 1, 3.

Mosley, Don and Joyce Hollyday. "Come, Ye Disconsolate" *Sojourners* 25, no. 4 (July-August 1996) 22–25.

Nelson, Jr. Claud. "Why We Are 'Withdrawing from the World'" *Motive* March 1953, 11–14.

Page, Dan. "Martin and Mabel" *Baptists Today*, December 2004.

Pitzer, D. E. "Jordan, Clarence (1912–1969)." in *Dictionary of Baptists in America* (edited by Bill J. Leonard) Downers Grove, IL: InterVarsity, 1994.

"Religion: Embattled Fellowship Farm" *Time*, September 17, 1956.

"Rev. Clarence L. Jordan Dead; Led Interracial Farm Project" *New York Times*, October 31, 1969.

Shurden, Walter B. "Southern Seminary in the Life of the Southern Baptist Convention" *Review and Expositor* LXXXI, no. 4 (Fall 1984) 393–406.

Simmons, Paul D. "The Legacy of Clarence and Florence Jordan." Address given on the occasion giving The Clarence Jordan Award to Rev. Lincoln Bingham for his exemplary Christian service in Louisville and Jefferson County, 1992.

Snider, P. Joel. *The Cotton Patch Gospel: The Proclamation of Clarence Jordan* Lanham, MD: University Press of America, 1985.

Snider, Joel. "Hearing Parables in the Patch." *Christian Reflections* Center for Christian Ethics at Baylor University, 2006, 80–87.

Stricklin, David. "Clarence Jordan (1912–1969), Jasper Martin England (1901–1989) and Millard Fuller (1935–): Koinonia Farm: Epicenter for Social Change" in *Twentieth-Century Shapers of Baptist Social Ethics*, edited by Larry L. McSwain, 163–184. Macon, GA: Mercer University Press, 2008.

———. *A Genealogy of Dissent: Southern Baptist Protest in the Twentieth Century* Lexington: The University Press of Kentucky, 1999.

Strong, Douglas M. "Clarence Jordan (1912–1969): Creator of the 'Cotton Patch Gospel': Building Biblical Community." In *They Walked in the Spirit: Personal Faith and Social Action in America*, 91–106. Louisville, KY: Westminster John Knox, 1997.

Tillman, William M. "Clarence Jordan: Cotton Patch Prophet (1912–1969)." In *Baptist Prophets: Their Lives and Contributions*, 20–22. Brentwood, TN: Baptist History and Heritage Society, 2006.

Weiner, Kay N, ed. *Koinonia Remembered* Americus, GA: Koinonia Partners, 1992.

York, Tripp. "Clarence Jordan's Fellowship." In *Living on Hope While Living in Babylon*, 60–80. Eugene, OR: Wipf and Stock, 2009,\.

Clarence Jordan's Writings and Speeches

Hollyday, Joyce and Clarence Jordan. *Essential Writings* Maryknoll, NY: Orbis, 2003.

Jordan, Clarence. "As You Want People to Act Toward You." *The Church Advocate*, September 1967, 8-9.

———. "The Christian Community in the South" *Journal of Religious Thought* 14, no. 1, (Autumn-Winter 1956-1957) 27-36.

———. *Clarence Jordan's Cotton Patch Gospel: The Complete Collection*. Macon, GA: Smyth and Helwys, 2012.

———. *The Cotton Patch Version of Hebrews and the General Epistles*. New York: Association Press, 1973.

———. *The Cotton Patch Version of Luke and Acts*. Piscataway, NJ: New Century, 1969.

———. *The Cotton Patch Version of Matthew and John*. New York: Association Press, 1970.

———. "Dear President Eisenhower." January 22, 1957.

———. "Draft the Boys at 65" *Bruderhof Communities*, 2004.

———. "The Good Samaritan." *Mennonite Life*, January 1967, 17-18.

———. "Here is the Church." (audio mp3 file) Koinonia Partners. Online: http://www.koinoniapartners.org/clarence/sounds/heristhechurch.mp3.

———. "Impractical Christianity." *Sunday School Young Peoples' Quarterly*, Third Quarter 1948, 2.

———. "In the Land of Great Violence" *The Mennonite* 25 (May 1965) 353.

———. "Is It an Impossible Job?" *Young People* 12 (August 1956) 9-10.

———. "Is Non-Violence Enough?" *Baptist Leader*, February 1964, 12-13.

———. "Jesus and Possessions." In *Kingdom Building: Essays from the Grassroots of Habitat* edited by Robert William Stevens and David Johnson Rowe. Americus, GA: Habitat for Humanity, 1984.

———. "Learn to Take It on the Chin" *The Church Advocate*, August 1966, 8-9.

———. *The Letter to God's People in Washington or Romans* in *The Koinonia Cotton Patch Version*. Americus, GA: Koinonia Farm, 1968.

———. *Letters to God's People in Columbus (Colossians) and Selma (I and II Thessalonians)*, in *The Koinonia Cotton Patch Version*. Americus, GA, Koinonia, 1967.

———. "Letter to President Eisenhower." January 22, 1957.

———. "Love Your Enemies" *Post-American* 2 (May-June 1972) 4-5.

———. "The Meaning of Christian Fellowship." *Prophetic Religion* 7 (Spring 1946) 3-6.

———. "The Meaning of Thanatos and Nekros in the Epistles of Paul" Unpublished Doctoral Dissertation, Southern Baptist Theological Seminary Louisville, Kentucky, 1938.

———. "One Jesus for Another" *Christian Living*, October 1965, 20-22.

———. "A Parable of No Violence, Some Violence, and Great Violence." *Town and County Church*, November-December 1965, 9.

———. "Peace and Brotherhood" *Koinonia Peace and Justice*, Baptist Peace Fellowship, Detroit MI, May 19, 1963.

———. "A Personal Letter to Friends of Koinonia Farm." *The Church Advocate*, July 1969, 12-13.

———. *Practical Religion or, the Sermon on the Mount and the Epistle of James*, in *The Koinonia Cotton Patch Version*. Americus, GA: Koinonia Farm, 1964.

———. "Racial Frontiers." *Baptist Student*, November 1941, 6-7.

———. "The Rich Farmer." *The Presbyterian Outlook*, March 27, 1967, 4.
———. "The Sound of a Dove." *Town and Country Church*, 1961, 16.
———. *The Substance of Faith and Other Cotton Patch Sermons*, edited by Dallas Lee. Eugene, OR: Cascade Books, 2005.
———. *Sermon on the Mount* Valley Forge, Pennsylvania: Judson Press, 1952.
———. "Things New and Old." In *Peace and Nonviolence* edited by Edward Guinan, 114–120. New York: Paulist, 1973.
———. "When Jesus Came to Georgia" *The Church Advocate*, February 1967, 8–9.
———. *Why Study the Bible?* Philadelphia: Baptist Youth Fellowship, 1953.
Jordan, Clarence and Bill Lane Doulos *Cotton Patch Parables of Liberation* Scottdale, PA: Herald, 1976.

Clarence Jordan and Friends Speeches and Interviews

Included are examples of Clarence Jordan's speeches or presentations about Clarence Jordan and Koinonia Farm. Materials listed include places where the items can be found. Materials that can be purchased from the Koinonia catalog are marked with the letter "K." Some items can also be found in Southern Baptist Theological Seminary Library (SBTS) and Bethel Seminary (BS).

Records

Jordan, Clarence. "The Great Banquet and Other Parables." Tiskilwa, IL: Koinonia Records, nd. (BS)
———. "Jesus the Rebel and Jesus and Possessions." Evanston, IL: Koinonia Records, nd.
———. "Metamorphosis and Love Your Enemies." Evanston, IL: Koinonia Records, nd.
———. "The Rich Man and Lazarus and Other Parables retold for Our Times." Evanston, IL: Koinonia Records, nd. (BS)
———. "Judas." Evanston, IL: Koinonia Records, nd.

Tapes/CDs

Jordan, Clarence. "Christian Pacifism/Draft the Boys at 65." (CD/K)
———. "Christians Under Pressure." (3 cassettes) Americus, GA: Koinonia Records. (BS)
———. "The Cotton Patch Parables: A Bible Study for Thinking Christians." (4 CD set with study guide) Americus, GA: Koinonia Records. (CD/K)
———. "Episodes from Acts." (2 cassettes) Americus, GA: Koinonia Records. (BS)
———. "Great Banquet/Angry Banker and Rich Farmer/Buried Treasure." (1 cassette) Americus, GA: Koinonia Partners, nd. (BS)
———. "Incarnating Brotherhood" Americus, Georgia: Koinonia Records (BS)

———. "Jesus the Rebel and Jesus and Possessions." (1 cassette) Americus, GA: Koinonia Partners, nd. (BS)
———. "Judas and The Man from Gadera." (1 cassette). Americus, GA: Koinonia Partners, nd. (BS)
———. "Metamorphosis and Love Your Enemies." (1 cassette). Americus, GA: Koinonia Partners, nd. (BS)
———. "The Koinonia Story." Americus, GA: Koinonia Partners, nd. (CD/K)
———. "Power from Parables." (4 cassettes) Americus, GA: Koinonia Records. (BS)
———. "The Prodigal Son, Rich Man and Lazarus, and The Good Samaritan." (1 cassette). Americus, GA: Koinonia Partners, nd. (BS)
———. "Man of Faith: Selections from Jordan's Sermons and Lectures." Americus, GA: Koinonia Partners, nd.
———. "The Sabbath as a Way of Life." (1 cassette). Americus, GA: Koinonia Records. (BS)
———. "Living the Sermon on the Mount." Recorded at the American Baptist Conference Center in Green Lake Wisconsin. (BS)
———. "Substance of Faith." (1 cassette). Americus, GA: Koinonia Records. (BS)
Morrison, Scott "Clarence Jordan Interview." Americus, GA: Koinonia Partners, nd. (CD/K)

DVD's and VHS and Relevant Supporting Materials

Briars in the Cottonpatch: The Story of Koinonia Farm. Cotton Patch Productions, 2003. (DVD/K)
Cotton Patch Gospel (Tom Key). DVD. Bridgestone Productions, 1988. (K)
Cotton Patch Gospel (Tom Key). (CD). (K)
Staggs, Al. "Clarence Jordan and the God Movement." (DVD). (K)
———. "Role Models for Walking the Talk in the 21st Century." *American Baptist News Service,* July 1, 2009.
Synopisis of "Briars in the Cotton Patch" *Georgia Public Broadcasting,* February 2005.
"Tom Key Looks Back." Dramatic Publishing 2004.
Westmoreland-White, Michael L. "Al Staggs: Baptist Minister and Acts for the Kingdom." *Levellers* July 31, 2007.

Audiovisual materials on Clarence Jordan at Southern Baptist Theological Seminary Library, Bethel Seminary Library and Other Sites

Barnette, Henlee H. and Frank Stagg. "Chapel Address, November 19, 1969: Memorial Service for Clarence Jordan" Southern Baptist Theological Seminary, Louisville, Kentucky (audiobook Reel-to-reel) (SBTS)
Barnette, Henlee H. "Chapel Address" April 6-7, 1982" Louisville, Kentucky: Southern Baptist Theological Seminary, 1982. (cassette) (SBTS)
———. "Clarence Jordan" March 13, 1984 Ethics Luncheon Southern Baptist Theological Seminary 9 (cassette) (SBTS)

Finlator, William Wallace. "Chapel Address: Clarence Jordan and the Bible" April 19, 1983, (Recorded in Alumni Memorial Chapel, Southern Baptist Theological Seminary. (cassette) (SBTS)

———. "Clarence Jordan and Economic Issues." April 20, 1983, Chapel Address Southern Baptist Theological Seminary (cassette) (SBTS)

Jamison, Gayla. "Enough to Share a Portrait of Koinonia Farm. Southern Baptist Theological Seminary, 1983. (video) (SBTS)

Jordan, Clarence. "Ancient Men with a Modern Twist" Bethel College Bible Lectures February 2-5, 1969. (cassette)

———. "Chapel Address: The Humanity of God," October 2, 1968, Southern Baptist Theological Seminary, Louisville, Kentucky) (cassette) (SBTS)

———. "Chapel Address, 1983, April. 20: Clarence Jordan and Economic Issues." Recorded in Alumni Memorial Chapel, Southern Baptist Theological Seminary. (cassette) (SBTS)

———. "Christianity as a Movement" (audio mp3 file). Koinonia Partners. Online: http://www.koinoniapartners.org/clarence/sounds/christianitymovement.mp3.

———. "Classroom Lecture." Recorded at Southern Baptist Theological Seminary October 2, 1968. (cassette) (SBTS)

———. "Lecture: On Nonviolence." Southern Baptist Theological Seminary October 1, 1968. (SBTS)

———. "Power in the Parables." Bethel College Bible Lectures, February 2-5, 1969.

———. "Spiritual Discipline." Southern Baptist Theological Seminary, 1959. (SBTS)

Jordan, Florence. "Koinonia Today: With Discussion Questions." Recorded at Southern Baptist Theological Seminary, 1982–1983. (cassette) (SBTS)

———. "Classroom Lecture." Southern Baptist Theological Seminary, April 19, 1983. (SBTS)

———. "Classroom Lecture." Southern Baptist Theological Seminary, May 3, 1974. (SBTS)

Pratt, Kris. "Justice in the Cotton Patch: Clarence Jordan on Economic and Racial Justice." (audio recording) CBGNC General Assembly, March 25, 2011.

Ragsdale, Vicki. "Interview of Florence Jordan." Recorded in the Southern Baptist Theological Seminary Television Studio, March 18, 1986, (video) (SBTS)

Simmons, Paul D., et al. "Interviews About Clarence Jordan: Paul Simmons interviews Dale Moody and Peyton Thurman About the life of Clarence Jordan and His Work as Founder of Koinonia Farms." Recorded in the Southern Baptist Theological Seminary Television Studio, 1980. (video) (SBTS)

Thurman, William, et al. "Chapel Address, April 29, 1981, Reflections on Clarence Jordan." (audiobook cassette) Alumni Memorial Chapel, Southern Baptist Theological Seminary (SBTS)

Selective Habitat for Humanity and Millard and Linda Fuller Writings and Speeches

Baggett, Jerome P. *Habitat for Humanity: Building Private Homes, Building Public Religion.* Philadelphia: Temple University Press, 1960.

Bryant, John Hope. "A Legend, Habitat for Humanity Founder Millard Fuller Dies." *johnhopebryant.com* February 5, 2009. Online: http://www.johnhopebryant.com/

john_hope_bryant_/2009/02/a-legend-habitat-for-humanity-founder-millard-fuller-dies.html.

Carter, Jimmy. "Interview with Millard Fuller." *ChristianEthicsToday* 4 (December 1995) 6.

Clemens, Steve. "Remembering Millard: My Reminiscing About Millard Fuller." *FullerCenter.org*, March 19, 2009. Online: http://www.fullercenter.org/news/Remembering-my-dad-Millard-Fuller-by-georgia-fuller-luedi.

"A Conversation with Millard Fuller" *Single Adult Ministries, Journal* March 1998, 9–11.

Frykholm, Amy. "One House At a Time" *Christian Century* December 16, 2008, 10–11.

Fuller, Millard. *Beyond the American Dream* Macon, GA: Smyth and Helwys, 2010.

———. *Building Materials for Life, Volume I*. Macon, GA: Smyth and Helwys, 2002.

———. *Building Materials for Life Volume II*. Macon, GA: Smyth and Helwys, 2004.

———. *Building Materials for Life Volume III*. Macon, GA: Smyth and Helwys, 2007.

———. *Bokotola*. New York: Association Press, 1977.

——— *The Excitement is Building*. Waco, TX: Word, 1990.

———. "A House is a Sermon of Christ." *Eternity*, September 1997, 44–45.

———. "An Interview with Millard Fuller." *Christian Ethics Today* 4, December 27, 2010.

———. (with Diane Scott) *Love in the Mortar Joints*. Piscataway, NJ: New Century, 1980.

———. *More Than Houses: How Habitat for Humanity is Transforming Lives and Neighborhoods*. Waco, TX: Word, 2000.

———. *No More Shacks!* Waco, TX: Word, 1986.

———. "Quiet Heroes: Building a Life." *Christian Networks Journal* (Winter 2002) 14–15.

———. *A Simple, Decent Place to Live: The Building Realization of Habitat for Humanity*. Dallas, TX: Word, 1995.

———. *Theology of the Hammer*. Macon, GA: Smyth and Helwys, 1994.

Fuller, Millard and Linda Fuller. *The Excitement is Building*. Dallas: Word, 1990.

Gailard, Frye. *If I Were a Carpenter: Twenty Years of Habitat for Humanity*. John F. Blair, 1996.

Goodrich, Chris. *Faith is a Verb*. Brookfield, CT: Gimlet Eyes, 2005.

Hayes, Kathleen. "Interview with Millard Fuller." *Other Side*, January 1986, 12–15.

Hinson, David and Justin Miller. *Designed for Habitat*. London: Routledge, 2012.

Korthase, Sherry C. "Millard Fuller (1935–2009)." *The New Georgia Encyclopedia*, February 5, 2009.

Lewis, Gregg. "Linda and Millard Fuller" *Marriage Partnership* Spring 1990, 38–40.

Lyman-Barner, Kirk. "What the Poor Need is Not Charity, But Capital. So, What Do the Rich Need?" *The Fuller Center*, January 28, 2011.

Martin, Douglas. "Millard Fuller, 74, Who Founded Habitat for Humanity, Is Dead." *New York Times*, February 4, 2009, 28.

Maudlin, Michael. "God's Contractor." *Christianity Today*, June 14, 1999, 44–47.

"Millard Fuller, 1935–2009: Habitat Founder Remembered as Visionary." *Christian Century*, March 10, 2009, 17.

Pierce, John. "Master Builder for God: Remembered Simply." *Baptists Today*, February 4, 2009.

———. "Millard, Socks and the Taser Guy." *Baptists Today*, October 26, 2009.

Shor, Fran. "Hammerin' on Heavens Door" *New Politics*, Winter 2008, 65–70.

Stafford, Tim. "How to Build Homes Without Putting Up Walls." *Christianity Today*, June 10, 2002.

Stelten, Gene G. *Thanks Mom! A Collection of Stories and Artwork to Benefit Habitat for Humanity*. Atlanta, GA: Peachtree, 1999.

Schwartz, Bob. "Millard Fuller and Clarence Jordan." *Religion Report*, February 4, 2009.
Starling, Kelly. "Habitat for Humanity" *Ebony*, November 1997, 200–207.
Vande Koppelle, Robert P. *The Invisible Mountain: A Journey of Faith* Eugene, OR: Wipf and Stock, 2010.
Willimon, William H. "Millard Fuller's Theology of the Hammer." *Christian Century*, October 5, 1988, 862–863.
Youngs, Bettie B. *The House That Love Built*. Charlottesville, VA: Hampton Road, 2007.

Materials and Responses to Clarence Jordan Symposium

Allen, Bob. "Jimmy Carter fetes Clarence Jordan" *abpnews*, October 11, 2012. Onine: http://www.abpnews.com/ministry/people/item/7883-jimmy-carter-fetes-clarence-jordan.
———. "Koinonia Farms Plans Clarence Jordan Symposium" *abpnews*, July 31, 2012. Online: http://www.abpnews.com/ministry/people/item/7665-koinonia-farms-plans-clarence-jordan-symposium
Carey, Greg "Recalling Clarence Jordan, Radical Disciple." *huffingtonpost.com*, June 3, 2012. Onine: http://www.huffingtonpost.com/greg-carey/clarence-jordan-radical-disciple_b_1548373.html.
Carlson, G. W. "Clarence Jordan: Celebrating a Conscientious Christian Dissenter." *The Pietist Schoolman,* August 16, 2012. Onine: http://pietistschoolman.com/2012/08/16/clarence-jordan-celebrating-a-conscientious-christian-dissenter/.
———. "Reflections on the Clarence Jordan Symposium." *The Pietist Schoolman*, December 20, 2012. Online: http://pietistschoolman.com/2012/12/20/reflections-on-the-clarence-jordan-symposium-g-w-carlson/.
Cep, Casey N. "Christ in the Cotton Patch: Clarence Jordan and the Koinonia Farm." *huffingtonpost.com*, November 19, 2012. Online: http://www.huffingtonpost.com/casey-n-cep/clarence-jordan-and-koinonia-farm_b_1967749.html.
Claiborne, Shane. "Happy Birthday Clarence!" *redletterchristians.org*, July 28, 2012. Online: http://www.redletterchristians.org/happy-birthday-clarence/.
Claiborne, Shane and Jonathan Wilson Hartgrove, "Remembering Clarence Jordan." Vimeo October 5, 2012. Online: http://vimeo.com/50543018
"Clarence Jordan: The Man Who Inspired the Fullers' Affordable Housing Movement." *Fuller Center for Housing*, July 27, 2012. Online: http://www.fullercenter.org/news/Clarence-Jordan-The-man-who-inspired-the-Fullers-affordable-housing-movement
Clemens, Steve. "Remembering Clarence Jordan on 100 Anniversary of His Birth." *Mennonista*, 2012. Online: http://mennonista.blogspot.com/2012/07/remembering-clarence-jordan-on-100th.html.
Fossum, Christy. "Koinonia Farm and Clarence Jordan Celebration." *sundaybysunday withchristy* October 4, 2012. Online: http://sundaybysundaywithcristy.blogspot.com/2012/10/koinonia-farm-and-clarence-jordan.html.
Gatlin, Joe. "All Things in Common." *Habitat World*, August 2012. Online: http://www.habitat.org/lc/hw/archived/stories/all-things-common/.
Gregg, Carl. "From Independence Day to Interdependence." *patheos.com*, July 3, 2012. Online: http://www.patheos.com/blogs/carlgregg/2012/07/from-independence-day-to-interdependence/.

Harvey, Paul. "Interracialism and Christian Community in the Postwar South: Clarence Jordan, Southern Baptist Visionary." *usreligion.blogspotcom*, August 12, 2012. Online: http://usreligion.blogspot.com/2012/08/interracialism-and-christian-community.html.

Hearne, Joshua. "Clarence Jordan, Farmer, Founder of Koinonia Farm, Opponent of the Status Quo" *Telling Stories that Matter*, October 27, 2012. Online: http://www.ttstm.com/2010/10/october-27-clarence-jordan-farmer.html

Hodges, Sam. "The Enduring Influence of Clarence Jordan" the *United Methodist Reporter*, September 15, 2012.

Johnson, Chris. "Clarence Jordan at 100: An Influential Soul." *Fuller Center for Housing* 2012.

———. "Clarence Jordan: The Man Who Inspired the Fullers' Affordable Housing Movement." *The Fuller Center*, July 27, 2012. Online: http://www.fullercenter.org/news/Clarence-Jordan-The-man-who-inspired-the-Fullers-affordable-housing-movement.

———. "Simple Way's Shane Claiborne brings Fuller Center to Philadelphia." *Fuller Center for Housing*, November 30, 2012. Online: http://www.fullercenter.org/news/Simple-Way's-Shane-Claiborne-brings-Fuller-Center-to-Philadelphia.

Kaylor, Brian. "Happy Birthday Clarence" *blog.briankaylor.com*, July 29, 2012. Online: http://blog.briankaylor.com/2012/07/happy-birthday-clarence.html.

Kohls, Gary G. "Clarence Jordan, Conscientious Objector to War and Killing: More Lessons From the History of American Fascism, Racism, Militarism, and Economic Oppression." *duluthreader.com*, June 22, 2012. Online: http://duluthreader.com/articles/2012/06/22/656_clarence_jordan_conscientious_objector_to_war_and.

Lyman-Barner, Kirk. "Clarence Never Said: 'Nothing Can Be Done.'" *koinonia2012celebration.org* July 27, 2012. Online: http://www.koinonia2012celebration.org/clarence-never-said-nothing-can-be-done/.

———. *Koinonia Farm 2012 Celebration: Commemorative Program September 28-29, 2012*. Americus, GA: A Koinonia Publication, 2012.

———. "A Ride on the Love Train." *The Fuller Center for Housing*, March 16, 2012. Online: http://fullercenter.org/blog/10?page=1.

McBrayer, Ronnie. "A Demonstration Plot: Remembering Clarence Jordan, Part 1 of 3" *blog.beliefnet.com*, September 2012. Online: http://www.beliefnet.com/columnists/keepingthefaith/2012/09/a-demonstration-plot-remembering-clarence-jordan-part-1-of-3.html.

———. "Help Us Ship the Nuts Out of Georgia—Remembering Clarence Jordan, Part 2 of 3" *blog.beliefnet.com*, September 2012. Online: http://www.beliefnet.com/columnists/keepingthefaith/2012/09/help-us-ship-the-nuts-out-of-georgia-remembering-clarence-jordan-part-2-of-3.html.

———. "In Scorn of Consequences—Remembering Clarence Jordan, Party 3 of 3" *blog.beliefnet.com*, September 2012. Online: http://www.beliefnet.com/columnists/keepingthefaith/2012/09/in-scorn-of-the-consequences-remembering-clarence-jordan-part-3-of-3.html.

Millstein, Ezra. "All Things in Common." parliamentofreligions.org September 19, 2012.

Nelson-Munson, Pamela. "Stripping Down to God." Ashland, OR: First United Methodist Church, October 14, 2012.

Pierce, John. "Loving Respect, Clear Disagreement" *Baptists Today*, April 30, 2012.

———. "Vincent Harding: 'Keeper of a Story'" *Baptists Today*, April 30, 2012.

Seat, Leroy. "Cotton Patch Saint Committed to Equality, Nonviolence." *ethicsdaily.com* August 1, 2012. Online: http://www.ethicsdaily.com/cotton-patch-saint-committed-to-equality-nonviolence-cms-19852.

———. "In Praise of Clarence Jordan." *theviewfromthisseat.blogspotcom* July 30, 2012. Online: http://theviewfromthisseat.blogspot.com/2012/07/in-praise-of-clarence-jordan.html.

Shenk, Joanna. "A Farm for the Kingdom." *Mennonite World Review*, July 9, 2012.

Staggs, Al. "Koinonia Farm 2012 Celebration." *Koinonia 2012*, July 27, 2012.

Swartz, Ted. "The Clarence Jordan Symposium." *tedandcompany.com* 2012. Online: http://www.tedandcompany.com/events/the-clarence-jordan-symposium/

Umstattd, Scott. "Clarence Jordan and Martin Luther King Jr.: Meeting in Albany Georgia." *Briars Documentary*, March 24, 2012. Online: http://briarsdocumentary.com/clarence-jordan-and-martin-luther-king-jr-meeting-in-albany-georgia//

Wilson-Hartgrove, Jonathan. "Clarence Jordan and God's Movement Today." *patheos.com* July 2, 2012. Online: http://www.patheos.com/blogs/jonathanwilsonhartgrove/2012/07/clarence-jordan-and-gods-movement-today/.

———. "Hope for the Future in Our Radical Past." *patheos.com* October 1, 2012. Online: http://www.patheos.com/blogs/jonathanwilsonhartgrove/2012/10/hope-for-the-future-in-our-radical-past/.

———. "21st Century Freedom Ride." *redletterchirstians.org* November 7, 2012. Online: http://www.redletterchristians.org/21st-century-freedom-ride/.

———. "The Truth About Community." *patheos.com* January 7, 2013. Online: http://www.patheos.com/blogs/jonathanwilsonhartgrove/2013/01/the-truth-about-community/.

Wood, George P. "Clarence Jordan Never Said, 'Nothing Can Be Done.'" georgewood.com July 30, 2012. Online: http://georgepwood.com/2012/07/30/clarence-jordan-never-said-nothing-can-be-done/.

Yoder, Kelli. "Looking for Heroes: Radical Activism Isn't Inspired at First Glance." *Mennonite World Review*, October 29, 2012.

Contributors

GREG CAREY is Professor of New Testament at Lancaster Theological Seminary and Resident Scholar for the Evangelical Lutheran Church of the Holy Trinity, Lancaster, Pennsylvania. In addition to other works, he is the author of *Sinners: Jesus and His Earliest Followers* (Baylor University Press, 2009) and *Ultimate Things: An Introduction to Jewish and Christian Apocalyptic Literature* (Chalice, 2005). His research explores early Christian social identity, the Synoptic Gospels, apocalyptic literature, and theological interpretation of the Bible. Greg regularly blogs for the *Huffington Post*: huffingtonpost.com/greg-carey.

G. W. CARLSON holds a BA from Bethel College and an MA and PhD in Russian history from the University of Minnesota. He has been a professor of history and political science at Bethel University since 1968. He regularly teaches a course on Christian nonviolence, which honors the work of Clarence Jordan and other Christian peacemakers. He is deeply committed to the Christian peace traditions, especially the values of the Anabaptist and Quaker heritages. He is the current editor of the *Baptist Pietist Clarion*. Carlson first encountered Clarence Jordan in 1963 when he was a student at Bethel College. He became an avid reader of the *Cotton Patch Gospels* and a strong advocate for the Koinonia Farm experiment. Carlson's peacemaking essays explore the kingdom commitments behind significant conscientious Christian dissenters, traits that often emerge from a recovered radical Anabaptist heritage.

JIMMY CARTER (James Earl Carter, Jr.), thirty-ninth president of the United States, was born October 1, 1924, in the small farming town of Plains, Georgia, just fifteen minutes from Koinonia Farm. He served as President of the United States from 1977 to 1981. Significant foreign policy accomplishments of his administration included the Panama Canal treaties, the Camp David Accords, the treaty of peace between Egypt and Israel, the SALT II treaty with the Soviet Union, and the establishment of U.S. diplomatic relations with the People's Republic of China. On the domestic side, the administration's achievements included a comprehensive energy program conducted by a new Department of Energy; major educational programs under a new Department of Education; and major environmental protection legislation. After leaving the Presidency, Carter became University Distinguished Professor at Emory University in Atlanta, Georgia and founded The Carter Center. He was awarded the Nobel Peace Prize in 2002 for his decades of untiring effort to find peaceful solutions to international conflicts, to advance democracy and human rights, and to promote economic and social development. President and Mrs. Rosalynn Carter have three sons, one daughter, twelve grandchildren, and six great-grandchildren. He is the author of twenty-five books, a long-time volunteer and supporter of Habitat for Humanity, and a Sunday School teacher at Maranatha Baptist Church in Plains, Georgia.

DR. ANN LOUISE COBLE was introduced to Clarence Jordan's book *Sermon on the Mount* as a teenager and eventually studied Jordan for her PhD dissertation at Saint Louis University. A native of Alabama, Coble now lives in Nashville and teaches religion at Belmont University. Her PhD dissertation was titled "A Demonstration Plot for the Kingdom of God: Koinonia Farm as Clarence Jordan's Incarnated Interpretation of the New Testament." A book version of her PhD dissertation was published in 2001 under the title *Cotton Patch for the Kingdom: Clarence Jordan's Demonstration Plot at Koinonia Farm*.

LINDA FULLER DEGELMANN and her late husband, Millard Fuller, spent a biblical forty years working together in the cause of making decent housing a reality for all of God's people. From their groundbreaking work with Clarence Jordan at Koinonia working with the Fund for Humanity's Partnership Housing, to their missionary call to Zaire, through the founding of Habitat for Humanity and The Fuller Center for Housing, Linda stood at Millard's side, hammer in hand, inspiring volunteers and new homeowners alike. Since Millard's death in 2009, Fuller Degelmann has stayed involved in the work, serving on the Board of Directors of The Fuller Center and sharing from her lifetime of ministry memories.

Contributors

For most of his twenty-two years of ministry before being elected Conference Minister of the United Church of Christ, Tim Downs served local congregations. He was committed to urban ministry and to the equipping of local congregations in urban settings to be "blessed communions, where we are opened to God's touch of grace, and opened to promise of transformation within our lives as a people of God." He understood local congregations as places where people are gathered to be healed, to be strengthened, and then to go forth for the "living of these days." As Conference Minister, Downs has been committed to the renewal of local congregations as a "basic unit of life and organization," and has understood that the United Church of Christ is most visible and present through the ministry of its local congregations.

VINCENT HARDING is an historian, author, and activist who has participated in movements for compassionate justice and nonviolent social change since the late 1950s. A friend and associate of Dr. Martin Luther King, Jr., Harding was active in the Southern Freedom (Civil Rights) Movement. Vincent was also a friend and associate of Clarence Jordan and arranged for the only in-person meeting between Jordan and King. Jordan requested the meeting to challenge King's use of boycott as a strategy in the civil rights movement. Harding was the founding director of both the Martin Luther King, Jr. Memorial Center and the Institute of the Black World, and is Professor Emeritus of Religion and Social Transformation at Iliff School of Theology.

JOYCE HOLLYDAY is a co-founder and co-pastor of Circle of Mercy, an ecumenical congregation in Asheville, North Carolina, where she lives in community on a small mountain farm. Hollyday is the author or editor of several books, including *Clarence Jordan: Essential Writings* (Orbis, 2003). She served for nine years as an Associate Conference Minister for the Southeast Conference of the United Church of Christ, and for fifteen years as the Associate Editor of *Sojourners* magazine. Her first feature article, written in 1978, was on the legacy of Clarence Jordan and Koinonia Farm.

DALLAS LEE is the author of *The Cotton Patch Evidence—The Story of Clarence Jordan and the Koinonia Farm Experiment* (Harper and Row, 1971), and editor of Clarence Jordan's transcribed extemporaneous lectures, *The Substance of Faith* (Association Press, 1972). His journalism career includes service as Southeast U.S. bureau chief for *The Associated Press*, city editor of *The Atlanta Journal-Constitution*, and associate editor of *Missions USA* magazine. He lives in Atlanta with his wife, Mary Carol.

SAM MAHONE was raised in Americus, Georgia. He joined the Student Non-Violent Coordinating Committee (SNCC) in 1962 and helped organize the Americus-Sumter County Civil Rights Movement of the 1960s. In 1984, Mahone opened the Ancestral Arts Gallery in midtown Atlanta to promote the work of local and national African American artists. Since 1997, Mahone has worked for the High Museum of Art. In 2007, Mahone helped found the Americus-Sumter County Movement Remembered Committee, Inc. (ASCMRC), which hopes to establish an Americus Civil Rights Museum and Interpretive Center to house memorabilia, photos, film, artifacts, and oral history.

CHARLES MARSH is Professor of Religious Studies and Director of The Project on Lived Theology at the University of Virginia. He is a graduate of Harvard Divinity School and the University of Virginia. The Project on Lived Theology research community seeks to understand the social consequences of religious beliefs. Shortly after publishing *Reclaiming Dietrich Bonhoeffer: The Promise of His Theology* (Oxford, 1994), Marsh began considering the religious and moral paradoxes of his southern Protestant upbringing. He was struck by the complex ways theological commitments and convictions came into dramatic conflict in the civil rights movement in the American South. The religious beliefs and social practices of ordinary people of faith illuminated a new way of writing theology for him, the first fruit being *God's Long Summer: Stories of Faith and Civil Rights* (Princeton, 1997), which won the 1998 Grawemeyer Award in Religion.

THE REVEREND DR. LEONORA TUBBS TISDALE is Professor of Homiletics at Yale Divinity School. She teaches the theory and practice of preaching, with research interests in congregational studies and preaching, women's ways of preaching, and prophetic preaching. She is the author or editor of eight books, including *Preaching as Local Theology and Folk Art, Prophetic*

Preaching: A Pastoral Approach. A former president of the Academy of Homiletics, Nora has served on the faculties of Union Theological Seminary in Virginia (now Union-PSCE) and Princeton Theological Seminary, and as adjunct faculty at Union Theological Seminary in New York. She also served on the pastoral staff of Fifth Avenue Presbyterian Church in New York City, where she provided theological oversight for the Center for Christian Studies, an innovative lay theological academy offering courses for over 2,000 people in the greater New York area.

DAVE WILLIS is a husband and dad living in northern New England. He's also a freelance writer and professional communicator working with associations, publishers, and businesses, primarily in insurance space.

GREG WITTKAMPER's family moved to Koinonia in July 1953, just before his sixth birthday. After graduating from Americus High in 1965, he spent four years as a student at Friends World College. The college, established by the Quakers as an experiment in world studies, made it possible for Wittkamper to travel to more than sixty countries around the world where comparative religion became his focus. Greg then worked as "Clerk of the Works" at the college for two years in lieu of alternative to military service. After traveling for another year he moved to "almost heaven" West Virginia and in 1976 began buying and selling real estate, which he still does on a part-time basis. Greg is also working with Jim Auchmutey on a book based on the experience of growing up at Koinonia Farm and going to public school, mainly Americus High School. He is married and has three children ages thirty-two, twenty-six, and ten.

www.ingramcontent.com/pod-product-compliance
Lightning Source LLC
Chambersburg PA
CBHW020850160426
43192CB00007B/861